POEMS TO READ WHILE DRIVING ON FREEWAYS

(AND OTHER WAYS TO DIE LAUGHING)

Paul Jeffrey Davids

POEMS TO READ WHILE DRIVING ON FREEWAYS (AND OTHER WAYS TO DIE LAUGHING)

First Edition (Revised) Published by
Yellow Hat Publishing
A Division of Yellow Hat Productions, Inc.
5190 Neil Road Suite #430
Reno, Nevada 89502

First Printing, May 2012

ISBN 978-0-9819244-2-7

I dedicate this collection to my wife, Hollace Davids, who has been immersed in all of my creative projects throughout the decades. I also dedicate this book to two of the biggest fans of my poetry: my mother, Frances Davids, who taught me to love literature when I was young, and to my sister, Jeanie Anne Dwyer, who inspired the poem BETTER HUG YOUR SISTER. I also include Rebekah Del Rio, a close friend and a remarkable singer, and two other creative confidants: Eva Fried and her mother, Lygia, who want to adopt ALBERT, THE ELEVATOR ALLIGATOR.

Acknowledgements

In addition to Hollace, I acknowledge and thank Brian Thomas Lambert, a brilliant musician who was present for the birth of Professor Hack HardDrive the day I first took on the alter ego of the professor in his music studio. Also, my sincere thanks to Russell and Martin Metzger. Our trip to Nashville together in Russell's truck to record music for my SCARLETT MAY BLOSSOM project led to my coming up with WE LOVE YOU, WE HATE YOU. And that, in turn, opened the floodgates to my writing all the other poems.

Foreword

What the world needs most today is not more oil and autos and high-rise skyscrapers and condominiums. What we need is more wit and whimsy. The severe shortage has caused bookstores to close, TV shows and movies to fail, and it has even caused candidates to lose elections, because most of them lack a sense of humor.

The international shortage of whimsical humor has even been known to cause indigestion, arthritis, wars, solar flares and even climate change.

If you want to compensate for this shortage, I do not recommend you take dietary supplements of whimsy sold in capsules in pharmacies and health food stores, because most of those products will not make you laugh – and generic whimsy supplements are filled with clichés.

Instead, I recommend that you stick to the major brand name. And by George, apparently you've found it, because you've begun reading POEMS TO READ WHILE DRIVING ON FREEWAYS (AND OTHER WAYS TO DIE LAUGHING)!

Table of Contents

1. POETRY IS DANGEROUS

In the hustle and bustle
Of the fast pace of modern life
Poetry is dangerous
Because it can make you think twice

No one wants to think twice
When thinking once will do
That's why people who read poetry
Number so very few

Poetry may wrap your mind
Around some obscure thought
How can there be any time for that?
With all the neat things you've bought!

And with so many social networks
And computers all online
Who is reading poetry?
Who possibly has time?

For in the hustle and bustle
Of urban life in a whirl
There's a choice you have made
Whether you are a boy or a girl

And if far off in the country
Is where you exist
Whether you be a man or a woman
You too have made the list

It's a list very long
With hundreds of millions
If we count the whole world
The list grows to billions

It is a list of all the names
Of those who refuse
To read any poetry at all
Because the mind it does confuse

They don't care if poetry is pretty
Like a flower in bloom
They don't care if poetry is witty
And can even carry a tune

With minds overburdened
By the videogame
It's no wonder that they're quite sure
That poetry is lame

And with their hours all filled
With both TV and the movie
It's a sure thing that they're quite sure
That poetry is not groovy

With all the time they spend angry
In traffic jams they can't stand
When it comes to reading poetry
There's not one single fan

And let's not forget
The most primary pleasure
Feasting leaves so few hours
For poetic leisure

There are other pleasures too
That I do not dare mention
This poem is not X-rated
That is not my intention

And with pods of all kinds
To carry around
With boom boxes and earphones
Which provide such loud sounds

POETRY IS DANGEROUS

There's one thing for sure
Of one thing there is no doubt
My message I won't scream
And I don't even have to shout

But I'll say it again
In case you forgot
Because you've been watching TV
Quite a lot

In the hustle and bustle
Of the fast pace of modern life
Poetry is dangerous
Because it can make you think twice

2. AIRPORT SECURITY

No problem is what I told the man
In his uniform so smart
X-ray me and pat me down
And excuse me if I fart

I apologize sincerely sir
For the penny in my pocket
That set off your security machine
With noise louder than a rocket

I took off my shoes and my belt
And my laptop I took out
My camera I removed for you
So you don't have to shout

I'm standing just where you told me
With my feet lined up just right
I swear that I don't have a bomb
Bombs give me quite a fright

A terrorist, me? Excuse me, sir
You suspect that I am one?
I didn't flunk out of high school
So believe me I'm not *that* dumb

I reached this splendid airport
Two – no, three hours ahead
So I could get through security
If I miss this plane I'm dead

I thought I'd have time to eat and read
And really enjoy my leisure
But I didn't count on that penny
Triggering this awful procedure

AIRPORT SECURITY

It's been an hour you've been checking me
For guns, explosives and knives
This pat-down is so thorough
I'm breaking out in hives

My pants are falling, my socks have holes
And I desperately have to pee
How many times must you check my groin?
Oh, sir, what are you *doing* to me?

3. THE SANTA MONICA FREEWAY

The Santa Monica Freeway deserves no blame
For all its rather infamous fame
That freeway really is rather tame
It's called Interstate Ten, remember that name

And there is no pleasure quite so divine
As driving south of Hollywood and Vine
On the Santa Monica Freeway, so sublime
But it was shut down after an earthquake for some time

With help from bureaucrats with white collars
Repaired it was for fifty million dollars
That splendid freeway that leads you and me
From Los Angeles downtown to the Pacific sea

Driving in morning rush hour is best
Because in the morning one is blessed
With lots of time to stop and stare
Because the traffic isn't moving anywhere

And if staring at accidents is your fancy
Opportunities many will you find
To witness smashups small and large
Cars crushed and mangled, every kind

The best part is near the four-oh-five
You'll come to a dead stop, but that's not sad
If endless meditation is your fancy
You'll attain nirvana and that's not bad

And if music is what you like best
You'll have a chance to put to the test
Every song on your iPod, every last one
Before the traffic jam is done

THE SANTA MONICA FREEWAY

Imagine drivers courteous, never mean
A freeway quite glamorous and ever so clean
Except for graffiti to the left and right
Or the pileup of bodies if there's a gory sight

Sooner or later you will need
To continue onward, so please proceed
Books on tape may help you think
If you don't mind smog – it might stink

If you're in a rush to get where you're going
Then night driving is for you, forget the day
At three a.m. it zips along in a hurry
Unless freeway repairs are underway

Do not talk on your cell phone
Unless you have Bluetooth, hands-free
Do not use the Diamond Lane
Unless you have passengers, one, two or three

For the fines you'll receive if you do cheat
Will exceed your taxes, so I'll repeat
If you are in the carpool lane and you're only one
Your time at the courthouse won't be fun

And contrary to the title of this book
If at this poetry you choose to look
While driving at any old speed
If you hit someone, you both may bleed

And if the freeway is under massive repair
And you see an obstruction, please don't text it
Or a police car will surely escort you
To the very next exit

Unless that exit proves to be blocked
And then on the freeway you are locked
So the cop will pull you over to the side
Where a ticket he'll give you with great pride

Paul Jeffrey Davids

Joyce Kilmer never saw a poem
As lovely as a tree
And Santa Monica, nowhere is there a freeway
As lovely as thee

4. ALBERT, THE ELEVATOR ALLIGATOR

Born was I an alligator
Far beneath a New York street
In the sewers was I bred and raised
My education was quite a feat

But refined am I, and learned
Vehicular studies have I read
I was born to end traffic congestion
So why do they want me dead?

My teeth they number many
Sharp as knives they are
No reflection on my intentions
Gentler am I by far
Than an upright, tranquil pony
Or a purring cat quite tame
Or a Golden Retriever loyal
Albert Alligator is my name

My skin it is quite coarse
The color rather green
Humans all misunderstand me
They consider me a creature mean

Do they realize how much I yearn?
I master all that I can learn
To someday ascend from far below
Directing traffic is all I know

Not like a cop who's on a beat
And not like policemen on the street
Using computers I've got the gumption
To really make New York function

For my destiny if fate there be
Is to work in Skyscraper Twenty-Three
Far above the toiling workers below
My office must be huge, you know

On floor seventy-five you'll see my devotion
To fix New York's problems of vehicle commotion
To create perfection of traffic control
Without ever charging a special toll

A specialist am I in urban mobility
My knowledge provides specialized utility
That I learned in the sewers so far below
Traffic is the discipline I really know

Sewers follow the path of each winding street
Every twist and turn, I know in my feet
And as above so it is below
I can save your drivers so much woe!

Of course I should serve this massive city
Giving all I have to the nitty gritty
Red lights, green lights, how they'll flow
Because I've figured out how to make traffic go

Yes, when I was born it was certainty
That an elevator alligator I was meant to be
With briefcase clutched between my jaws
I would scamper swiftly on all four paws

And before those elevator doors shall close
There are some questions I would like to pose
Your prejudice cruel does injure me
You are firmly set against admitting me
To your work force where I'd make a dollar
Even though I am without white collar
Why do you despise this alligator
Because he gets inside your elevator?

ALBERT THE ELEVATOR ALLIGATOR

Have I ever bitten any man?
And would I not stop to lend a hand?
If a hand I had that I could lend
If I could stand up and lean down to bend?

Every day a time clock I shall punch
With my snout so rumpled and long
And though I cannot sing at all
I have a weakness for human song

Especially music made to cater
To those who ascend the elevator
To work so hard on floor seventy-five
For all the days that they are alive

My mother loved me, never begged
That I conform when I left my egg
She knew I was not like other gators
Most of whom are people haters

She knew my talent as a technical director
And my gift for serving as traffic corrector
In wisdom did she nourish me
So people would all turn to me

And so as I scamper down the hall
To reach that elevator oh so small
Respect is all that I demand
Even if other alligators you cannot stand

For every being, whether big or small
If he has sharp teeth or none at all
Has a right to heed the inborn call
Of duty great, in spring or fall

So together upward we shall ride
That elevator with shared pride
In New York City that we know so well
The city Florida alligators think is hell

5. YOU'RE TRUE, YOU'RE FALSE

Thank goodness for honesty
And the man whose word is true
On him we can depend, that's sure
And I think that man is you

The truth is what you always tell
You never shade a single fact
You've never anything to sell
Your statements never lack

You trust that I can face it
You convey reality
You sometimes add a touch of wit
Because you're close to me

But today you didn't tell it all
You must have been in a hurry
Today you told a lie to me
And that really makes me worry

Why did you start to make things up?
To paint a picture very rosy?
Do you think I don't deserve to know?
Do you think I'm just too nosy?

Now I can't believe a word you say
Everything could be all made up
You've such a knack for fiction
I think you really suck

You've left me so depressed
My entire world you've rocked
I don't know if you're true or false
You've gone off so half-cocked

YOU'RE TRUE, YOU'RE FALSE

I think you lie just all the time
You are not what you claim
You lie and then you lie again
It's you who is to blame

I've lost my faith, what will I do?
I've really got to get over you
I'm so confused, I've lost my way
I just can't go on another day

But wait, perhaps your faults I've listed
Aren't really true, perhaps *I'm* twisted
Quite possibly I got it wrong
And you spoke the truth… all along?

Perhaps in my state of confusion
I've jumped to a conclusion
I see it now, the truth is clear
Everything you whisper in my ear
Is really true
I do love you
Because your word is true

I know it now, you're good as gold
I accept you back into the fold
Forgive my doubt that was so severe
I pushed you away with hate and fear

My behavior makes me want to cry
Now I'll believe you until I die
You're honestly true and truly honest
Except for when you lie

Yes, you're honestly true and truly honest
Except for when you lie

6. THE MAN WITH NO NAME

There was a man who spoke plain
But he could not remember his name
Try as he might, it was always a fight
But his name never came to light

The problem was worst at a party
Filled with guests who were all rather arty
He'd smile at each and his mind he'd beseech
But his name remained out of reach

A huge moral crisis ensued
How would his silence be construed?
Each guest knew his own name, that much was plain
And this man had his own memory to blame

It is awkward right now that I call him "this man"
But to call him otherwise, well nobody can
As a worst case one could invent a name
But that would commence a terrible game

For lies and deception lead only to ill
And our man was a man of decided good will
He knew not what to do, so he took off his left shoe
And as his guilt grew and grew, madness did ensue

So with that shoe he struck his own head
And he nearly fell down absolutely quite dead
But death was not to be, as everyone could see
And the bump on his head he did dread

Suddenly he found a firm voice
To speak to one and all was his choice
He thrust out his chest, ignoring all the rest
And he shouted "My name is Royce!"

THE MAN WITH NO NAME

But was it, you see, really meant to be
That his name would reveal itself so easily?
He tossed it around without making a sound
And then stammered "No, my name is Lee"

But of course it was neither Royce nor Lee
Nor Tom nor Harold nor George nor Henry
Nor Bob nor Bill, was he over the hill?
Was that the reason his memory was nil?

His right shoe he then did remove
His mind was quite out of groove
Was he Kenneth or Andrew or Kyle?
He was in a panic now all the while

The right shoe struck his brow with full force
And he tumbled right over, of course
There was nothing to do but claim that he knew
His entire name from its source

From his wallet in great frustration
He took out his car registration
But it had no name, how could that be?
Was it possible he had no family tree?

"It says right here," he did lie
While all of the guests did sigh
"Here is my name, I'm a man of great fame
And my memory lapse I now can tame"

The crowd was in quite a hush
Suspense mounted, they wanted to bust
"What is your name, oh please tell us your name!"
For this man all the women felt lust

Said he: "I will tell you the truth right now
And all of you will gasp with a WOW
When you know who I am, that my name is Sam
And related to each, your trust I beseech

For your Uncle am I
How I want to cry
For your nation and I
Are one and the same
No wonder I couldn't
Remember my name
I've lost my way
Yesterday and today
With myself I do war
Because I was great before
But now I've sunk low
I've a tough path to hoe
Please forgive me one and all
I've had a great fall
For I am your Uncle Sam
That indeed is who I am"

The guests all looked very perplexed
And some were even quite vexed
The audacity shown
Was quite overblown
How could this man claim
That Uncle Sam was his name?
Uncle Sam had great station
Uncle Sam is our nation
Uncle Sam does no wrong
It says so in the song
The star spangled flag
Is certainly no rag
And this man gone half mad
Was assuredly bad

Suddenly they all wanted to kill
That was their terrible will
Could they shoot him or hang him
Or hack him or whack him?
Could they stab him in violent fits?
Or simply blow him to bits?

THE MAN WITH NO NAME

So Uncle Sam suddenly did run
That party was certainly not fun
And then suddenly his name appeared in a flash
While he was making a forty yard dash
How could he have acted so very rash?
Uncle Sam was going bankrupt, running out of cash
Uncle Sam was not who he was at all
He had a faint inkling his name was Paul

"I am Paul," he declared – then, "no, not Paul at all
I am Charles Montgomery Livingston Saul
No, that's not who I am, that's not who I am
I'm Elvis Goliath Boy George the Third of Siam
J. C. Penny J. Edgar the son of Jack Benny
Paul McCartney Ringo, the son of Kenny
Loggins and Messina and the Bee Gees too"
Well, if that was his name what was he to do?

He turned to his wife, in fear of his life
Her stare was sharp, like the point of a knife
Yes, his wife was fit to be tied
As she sternly took him aside
"Your name is Paul Smith, so be done with it
Go home to bed, and don't strike your head
To be a Smith – well, one can make a case
That it is certainly no disgrace
A million Smiths there are
Who live near and far
And as far as being Paul
Don't stumble and fall
Just admit who you are
And then drive your car
Home for the night
And under covers quite tight
Begin to dream
That you are not who you seem

Paul Smith then said with much passion
In a very declarative fashion:
"I'd prefer no name at all
Than a name like Paul
And as for the Smith
I cannot live with it
With a name that's so dull
In my spirit there's no lull
Just turmoil and pain
I'll never be the same
So I'll still rack my brain
In sunshine, snow or rain
I'll be he who can't remember his name
Yes in sunshine
And snow
And also in rain
I'll be the man who can't remember his name"

7. YOU'RE THINNER, YOU'RE FATTER

You're thinner, much thinner
That's really good news
Your old clothes now fit you
Say goodbye to the blues

Congratulations, my friend
You're the picture of health
You've achieved something
Much better than wealth

You've lost thirty pounds
And you look so thin
You've even lost
That double chin

Your diet's a smash
Counting calories has saved you
How much better you look
Your body's brand new

You learned the techniques
Mastered every system
Those pounds melted away
And you'll never miss them

So come on my friend, let's go celebrate
The fact that you've lost all that weight
Let's take a bite of this chocolate cake
And a few of those cookies your did bake

You're thinner, you're fatter
You're fatter, you're thinner
You're thinner, you're thinner
You're thinner

Paul Jeffrey Davids

A year has passed
But it's been a disaster
You're up forty pounds
You gained them back faster

Parties and dinners
And weddings and roasts
Booze in the blender
And too many toasts

You're fatter, much fatter
That's really bad news
You have no clothes that fit you
Say hello to the blues

You don't want to croak
So start a new diet
Buy low calorie foods
Go ahead and try it

Your will power is strong
You're strong as steel
Just eat twice a day
Give up a meal

Now give up two meals
And all of your snacks
That skinny ol' you
Is on its way back

The treadmill's your friend
Just keep movin'
You're back in shape
Life's really groovin'

You're thinner, much thinner
That's really good news
Your old clothes now fit you
Say goodbye to the blues

YOU'RE THINNER, YOU'RE FATTER

But now you slack off
You lose motivation
The pounds come back
It's an abomination

You're fatter than ever
You can't get through the door
You're out of breath
You can't jog any more

You're like a balloon
You can't even function
Better try surgery
You need liposuction

You need a new plan
Your life must be saved
Every time you see food
You ache and you crave

A lap band for your stomach
Will keep the food out
That will cure you at last
How can there be doubt?

Please put down that burger
Oh, you are deranged
The operation's tomorrow
It's all been arranged

You're fatter, much fatter
That's really bad news
You have no clothes that fit you
Say hello to the blues

But the surgery worked
Hip Hip Hooray!
You're shedding the pounds
And melting away!

Paul Jeffrey Davids

You've learned a sad lesson
It's been really tough
Maintain a good weight
Or life will get rough

And if this doesn't convince you
Finally to eat right
Then it's time for farewell
And your last long goodnight!

8. TO HAVE OR HAVE NOT

This world it is full of Have-Nots
But there are Haves who bask in excess
Most of the Haves have never had not
But a few have what they have from success

Success is rare but some have it
It goes and it comes and it goes
The Have-Nots know not of success
What they have is a life full of woes

There are Have-Nots abundant whose wish
Is to halve the number of Haves and more
Sometimes they think that's the way to their goal
To increase the wealth of the poor

By halving the number of Haves right now
And spreading their wealth all around
And providing Have-Nots with assets thus gleaned
Would please many Have-Nots we have found

But the world hastens to have more Have-Nots
Who have not a prayer in hell
Of digging out of their debt and becoming Haves
And of learning to live quite well

And the Haves for their part
All they have they defend
Against those who would seize it
And the Haves' lives thus upend

The Haves all trust not
The government's long reach
Because high taxes leave Haves
Like whales on a beach

And there's inflation that steals
From the Haves who have much
And the wavering banks, sinking stocks
And the loss of equity and such

Everyone craves legal tender
But not all in this life have great splendor
Have-Nots and Haves we always shall have
Yes, that is the judgment I render

9. YOU'RE MARRIED, YOU'RE DIVORCED

You're married, my friend, you're married
Congratulations, tally-ho and godspeed
The bow in her hair and the ring that you wear
Prove you've got all you need

Oh, what a lucky day it is
You are betrothed, you are a whiz
Today was the day the knot you tied
Without ever really asking why

You are in love, or so you think
The roses prove it, white and pink
But maybe all's not what it seems
The way it was in your best dreams

A month or a year or a decade or so
In different directions you may grow
She to the left, you to the right
And once in a while you'll have a big fight

She'll kick and shout and call you a lout
You'll no longer beam, you'll rage and scream
And surely she'll lock you out of the room
You can no longer say that love is in bloom

You're divorced my friend, you're divorced
On this very terrible day
Life used to be swell and now it is hell
You're divorced my friend, you're divorced

But oh how quickly life can change
When a new woman comes to rearrange
The life that you had when alone you did settle
But now she will come to test your mettle

Another woman who is now in her prime
The new love of your life, it's all so sublime
And so back to the altar you do go
Without really knowing if she's friend or foe

She's sweet as can be, yes *that* you can see
And her dress is so white, it gives off such a light
Now you're married, my friend, married again
You're sure it's forever, without knowing there are ten
Yes, ten women will come and ten women will go
Your money they'll take and you'll be laid low
Marry again? Oh no, God forbid
There are *twelve* wives now of whom you are rid

But you'll do it again in a heartbeat so quick
If one great woman could make marriage stick
To marry again will do you no harm
Don't forget my friend, thirteen's the charm!

10. BETTER HUG YOUR SISTER

If great adventure is your plan
And you'll journey from the world you know
There is some advice you should consider
Before your problems grow

Before you depart on your adventure
Let your sister know she's keen
And that if all your plans should crumble
You still want her to share your dream

Because it's fine to climb high mountains
Or ford streams and rivers too
It's fine to live in the wilds
Where bears will be hunting you

It's nice to go aloft
In a big hot air balloon
It's fun to lose your way
And feel like a buffoon

Better yet, to fly your very own plane
Into lands that are still unknown
Going places where the natives
Have never seen a cell phone

And if those jungles call your name
And you drink wine from a carafe
While swinging high on Tarzan's vine
Staring at a huge giraffe

Or if outer space is your great fancy
And blasting off is your main game
Think of this poet's words
And how you'll never be the same
If you should forget those glory days
Growing up in your parents' home
When your sister could be so nice to you
And you never felt all alone

Before you climb aboard
Raft, balloon or spaceship
This old poet
Will give you a tip

Yes, wild brother, hear my plea
Clean out your ears, I'm speaking to thee
Before you go and completely blow it
A little love, you'd better show it

Being a big brother is truly special
When you long to rule the world
But when mosquitoes bite your neck
And the flag of failure has unfurled…

And when your raft has rudely capsized
Leading you to almost drown
When the jungle vine rips, then tears
And the gorillas all come around…

When your rocket ship
Runs out of gas
And you're trapped on the moon
Like a dumb jackass…

Or if cannibals surround you
And toss you into their stew
Remember your kid sister
Who always looked up to you

BETTER HUG YOUR SISTER

Yes, before your plans all fall apart
And you discover you really weren't so smart
And before that great adventure shall start
Remember the gal who is close to your heart

You know I'm talking about your sister
Don't forget how much you've missed her
You know you never should have dissed her
You'd better hug your sister!

11. YOU'RE HIRED, YOU'RE FIRED

Your resume? Terrific!
So you don't have to plead
You work with such great speed
You're the one we need!

We're thrilled that you will join us
You must feel mighty fine
You're perfect for our company
You showed up just in time

You're hired, my friend, you're hired
On this very glorious day
You're hired, my friend, you're hired
Yes, big checks we're gonna pay

Check out your huge office
You've nothing to lose!
Try out your big chair
Kick off your shoes

Pour some champagne
Let's all celebrate
This marvelous, wonderful
Fine twist of fate

You're hired, my friend, you're hired
On this very glorious day
You're hired and we're so wired
Big checks we're gonna pay

Don't hesitate to celebrate
This very fine twist of fate
We think you're great
And we cannot wait

YOU'RE HIRED, YOU'RE FIRED

But oh no, my friend
Wall Street's in a mess
Stocks are sinking
The banks are next

Let's take a deep breath
And try not to choke
Disaster has struck
We're going broke

You're fired, my friend, you're fired
On this very terrible day
You're fired, my friend, you're fired
Because it's you we cannot pay

It's time that you be on your way
Don't stay another day
Not even one more day
Because it's you we cannot pay

Yes, it's you we cannot pay
Indeed, you're the one we cannot pay

But now things are better
Come back to work!
Whoever fired you
That guy was a jerk

You've got your job back now
At least for a week
There's really good news
Unemployment has peaked

But the yen is down
And the dollar is up
Those folks over in Japan
are not buying our stuff

Paul Jeffrey Davids

And the national debt
Has gone to the moon
Oh no, you're laid off again
You came back too soon

You're fired, my friend, you're fired
On this very terrible day
One thing's for sure and one thing's true
It's you we cannot pay

So please just go away
You simply cannot stay
Because there are no jobs today
They've been outsourced far away

There's nothing to do but pray
Yes, get down on your knees and pray

If you wait for a year
Or make that two
Maybe by then
We'll have a new job for you

But until that day comes
You're in quite a stew
Unemployment will have to do
Yes, unemployment will have to do

12. THE SAGA OF JONAS SPOON

Jonas Spoon couldn't sing a tune
Nor build a barn nor run a farm
Nor build a fountain
Nor climb a mountain
Yes, Jonas Spoon couldn't sing a tune

But Jonas made a public testament
Describing a very sound investment
Horses would always carry man's load
Horses would take us down the road
Horses strong and with firm tail
Horses were sure to never fail

And so Jonas decided what to do
He bought ten thousand horseshoes new
He'd sell them all across the town
Across the state, and the whole world round
He'd make a profit very consequential
He'd become a horseman most influential
For there was one thing on which all agreed
Horses we would always need

But then one day driving down the main street
A new vehicle performed quite a feat
For this vehicle the church bells did peal
They called the thing an automobile

The noisy thing raised quite a fuss
And poor Jonas he did swear and cuss
The inventor Jonas wanted to feather and tar
Jonas despised that thing they called a car

He was sure its days would indeed be short
No respectable man would drive anything of that sort
It backfired and front-fired and rumbled loud
The horses hated it, they even cowed

Next door to Jonas a man named Able
Built a warehouse larger than a stable
And there Able manufactured tires and such
Things that horsemen would never touch

But demand for horseshoes slowed, then stalled
Jonas Spoon was quite appalled
There was no way the future he could alter
Man's love of cars just did not falter

Of the horseshoes very few were sold
Wretched and miserable Jonas did grow old
But he was not one to be outpaced
A new invention he embraced

With Samuel Morse one did not need a horse
Nor even need a car
To send a message through the air
To someone very far

The invention was the telegraph
Which relied upon Morse code
Dots and dashes and beeps and clicks
Morse code was the new mother lode

Better than smoke signals of Indian lore
Telegraph could send a message to your door
And so that clever Jonas Spoon did buy
A telegraph company, who could wonder why?

It was the invention of the age,
The invention of such a wise sage
Jonas spent every dime he ever earned
It was better than horseshoes, he had learned

THE SAGA OF JONAS SPOON

But there came a day when he wanted to stone
The man who invented the telephone
The telegraph soon was old hat
Nobody wanted any of that

For thanks to Alexander Graham Bell
They could talk by phone and all was well
And as for Morse code, it had no use at all
Because with telephones, everyone could call
Mother or father or brother, you know
Sister, aunt or uncle -- or friend or foe
All those telegraph clickers Jonah did buy
Were worthless, how he wanted to cry

Future inventions that seem only a fable
Show that the mind is more than able
To create a world that's more than it seems
To invent what only exists in dreams
And if in this story a lesson be
Around the corners of time, we cannot see

13. YOU'RE RIGHT, YOU'RE WRONG

We are quite infallible
Don't you know?
We cannot be wrong
For God says it's so!

And if with us
You do not agree,
We'll show you the light
And then you'll see

We are always certain
Of what we speak
If you think we're in error
Your nose we shall tweak

From the dawn of time
Everything that we've shown
Has been true and correct
And now it's all known

But oh gosh and oh my
You've got a good point
Maybe it's us
With a nose out of joint

You really are brilliant
So we're not going to pout
It's you who we trust now
There's really no doubt

Ever since you were born
There was no one like you
Whatever the question
It was you who knew

YOU'RE RIGHT, YOU'RE WRONG

We're so impressed
You are the very best
You score one hundred
On every test

We can't put up a fight
Because you're right
In the day you're right
And in the night

Never was a fellow
So sure of his mettle
You're right, you're right
You're right

We think you're entitled
To have a swelled head
There isn't a book
That you haven't read

If it's an answer we need
You'll do the deed
You're right, you're right
You're right

But what's that? Oh no!
You've made a mistake!
We thought you were perfect
But we see you're a fake

We counted on you
We were sure that you knew
But it's totally obvious
That you're human too

You don't know it all
So keep your eye on the ball
Since you're wrong after all
You'll have a great fall

Paul Jeffrey Davids

The mistake that you made
It's spoiled this poem,
You're wrong, you're wrong
You're wrong

Oh drat, there's another
Mistake that you've made
It's quite a pompous
Game that you've played

Making us think
With one clever wink
That you were the only one here
Who could think

But now we expect
You'll make another error
And for that very reason
We're living in terror

We played along
But our security's gone
You're wrong, you're wrong
Yes, horribly wrong

We ARE infallible
We always were
You were NEVER the one
To whom we should defer

We should have ignored you
And turned our back
For when it comes to brains
There's a lot that you lack

But gosh, no, you're right
It *is* us who's to blame
We got it all backwards
We've besmirched your fame

YOU'RE RIGHT, YOU'RE WRONG

You've proven that both
Of those errors we found
Were not errors at all
Because the world is *round*

The Earth it certainly *does*
Go around the sun
It spins in an orbit
That's your point and you've won

We thought it a fact
That the world was all flat
But you've proven it otherwise
And now that is that

14. JANET'S FLIGHT

Janet and her family of six or so
Were all excited as they set out for Chicago
They boarded a plane, it was a big jet
Their seats were together, they did not fret

A flight attendant, hair blond and eyes blue
Announced to all, and to Janet too
To the front of the plane and back, quite symmetrical
It was time to turn off everything electrical

Computers and cell phones and iPods and more
She was very strict about what was in store
The plane would take off high into the sky
But Janet was upset, she wanted to cry

She was busy listening to her favorite song
About outer space – thrills all the day long
Her iPod she absolutely refused to shut down
So the flight attendant gave her quite a frown

She said: "The captain insists you comply"
But she never gave a good reason why
She simply offered a general indication
That iPods interfered with communication

"Why, that's so silly," Janet cried out
"Don't disobey me," the attendant did shout
"Little girl you don't know the terrible danger"
Janet wrinkled her nose, this lady was stranger
Than her mother or teacher or Carla the maid
So all through takeoff her song she played
The attendant came back to take her iPod away
"You're endangering us all, you can't behave this way!"

JANET'S FLIGHT

You will not believe what happened next
Janet used her cell phone to try to text
To tell all her friends who were still on the ground
That the mean flight attendant hated the sound
Of Janet's favorite song, about a space ship
From deep out in space, where the Big Dipper does dip

The plane tipped and trembled and even did drop
Out of a cloud while Janet played rock
Then the plane took a detour, higher than before
And that's when the co-pilot opened his door

He walked over to Janet, scolding her loud
"Little girl you've caused our plane to fly above that cloud
Higher are we than we were ever meant to go"
"You amuse me," said Janet, "you put on such a show"

Then into outer space their plane did ascend
An airplane in outer space, that was a new trend
Her song she kept playing with its alien beat
A flying saucer approached, now that was quite neat

Suddenly a strange voice from the loudspeaker did call
Announcing weird greetings to one and to all
Outside the window, it was much blacker than coal
The poor captain was frantic, how this took quite a toll

The starlight shined in, and then a bright blinking light
From that flying saucer, a remarkable sight
"Greetings, Earthlings," said the strange voice with a twang
"We've heard Janet's song, it's one we all sang
On our planet afar, in the Big Dipper that dips
And so now your airplane will make a new trip
From your planet to ours, and then you'll return
Great sights you will see, and much you will learn"

The flight attendant, well – she was as mad as could be
"Janet, naughty child, now don't you see?
When the captain says turn off all electrical machines
If little girls won't listen, then our airplane careens
We go into orbit and then leave the planet
Oh, why must we have this passenger named Janet?"

Almost everyone enjoyed all they saw that day
Even though their plane went far out of its way
A new world they did visit, by faraway stars
Where funny folks lived who flew in odd cars

Cities of crystal and rivers of ice
Moons with great rings, they had to think twice
When they saw candy castles covered with fizz
And they realized how vast this universe is

Finally at last when they returned to Earth
Janet was filled with wonderful mirth
But the flight attendant was furious, filled with hate
Because to Chicago they arrived very late

15. YOU'RE RICH, YOU'RE POOR

Oh, you were so rich
You had so much money
You were so filthy rich
It's not even funny

But back when you started
It wasn't that way
Back in the day
You didn't roll in the hay

You started out poor
Not worth a cent
At the first of the month
You could not pay the rent

Yesterday's leftovers
Were all you could eat
You had holes in the shoes
That you wore on your feet

The jobs that you found
They paid you so little
The class that you were
Was not even middle

But then you got clever
You invented a Shmork
But all of your friends
Thought you were a dork

The Shmork it was popular
Everyone bought one
But they lasted one year
And then wouldn't run

Paul Jeffrey Davids

So folks bought another
And used that one up too
And royalties poured into
Your bank accounts new

You counted your money
From morning until night
The IRS wrote you
But you put up a fight

Your off-shore accounts
They grew and grew
You spent quite a lot
But saved a lot too

Buildings you bought
Warehouses and homes
Poor people called you up
Begging for loans

You cheated your friends
And your relatives too
You squeezed all your debtors
They were in a stew

But then came that lawsuit
So angry and fierce
Your patents were challenged
Your corporate veil pierced

The Shmork was not novel
You stole it they said
In spite of your wealth
You'd be better off dead

The lawyers defended you
At outrageous cost
The judge ruled against you
He declared that you lost

YOU'RE RICH, YOU'RE POOR

The money you had
You no longer owned
It was quite a crisis
You writhed and you moaned

And now you're a pauper
Like in the beginning
This sad game of life
You can't claim that you're winning

You're begging your friends
And your relatives too
Without their help
Whatever will you do?

But they do not know you
They've forgotten your name
And all that you had
The wealth and the fame
Vanished like dew
On a hot summer day
You cheated and lied
And now you will pay

You're finished, my friend
You're all washed up
Homeless, penniless
Down on your luck

But it's not all in vain
An idea has struck you
You'll have your revenge
On those people who screw you

Your new great idea
You've invented the Shmickle,
With all the money you'll make
You'll get out of this pickle

It works like a charm
And the patent you file
Puts you back on your feet
You win by a mile

Oh, you are so rich
You have so much money
You are so filthy rich
It's not even funny

Poverty's gone
A fortune you've made
Now forget about money
It's time to get laid

16. NOTHING IN PARTICULAR

First let me make it quite clear
To loved ones I consider dear
That in Particular for years there was nothing
Which is so remarkable, that's something

You are wondering –
How can a town be called Particular?
Well the reason in fact
Seems quite circular

It happened in a game
A game that wasn't tame
But a game it was, yes certainly
A game all the same

In a bar two gamblers with guns
With hands of poker gambled
And chattered and talked
In effect, they rambled

Their guns holstered
Their spirits bolstered
And with chips upon the table
Both of them were able
To talk over between them
The name of the town
But the talk led to anger
And a recurring frown

One owned a barn
The other owned a farm
They didn't get along
It was a cause for alarm

"You're not welcome in this town,"
Hank said to Chester in a tone unkind
"What town?" said Chester
"There's nothing here, are you blind?"

"Still, it should have a name,"
Said Hank who owned the barn
"Well, then I'll give it a name,"
Said Chester who owned the farm

"No me!" "No I!" "No me!" "No I!"
They argued till they dropped
They nearly drew their guns
But thank goodness they stopped

"I'll name it for my family,"
Said Hank who owned the barn
"No, I'll name it for MY family,"
Said Chester who owned the farm

"For a name there's none better
Than the name Particular,"
Said Chester, who in those parts
Was not very popular

"That's a very poor name for a town,"
Said Hank who owned the barn
"I admit you're Chester Particular
And you own a farm
But my name is Hank Lincoln
And Lincoln SOUNDS like a town
And if you move away
There'll be nobody named Particular around"

NOTHING IN PARTICULAR

Chester said that there already was
A place called Lincoln, a town
To name another town Lincoln
Would be the act of a clown

Well, the cards they did count
And the cards they did draw
And a dog wandered in
The dog raised his front right paw

"Well, now there's a dog in Particular,"
Chester did declare
The dog barked
He must have come from Somewhere

Somewhere was the town
That was just down the road
There was a pond in Somewhere
With many a toad

The dog had come from Somewhere
To be in Particular
The dog barked twice
His name was Molecular

Molecular distracted Hank
Who drew three cards face down
Hank shouldn't have done that
You could tell by his frown

So Chester won and got his way
And ever since that play
The town has been named Particular
Yes, ever since that famous day

The problem, though
That will certainly confound
Is that there's still nothing in Particular
Just no one around

Paul Jeffrey Davids

Unless you count the bar
But nobody does
Or the farm or the barn
Which aren't much because
A farm and a barn
Do not a town make
So from the very beginning,
It seemed that Particular was a mistake

That's when I leaped off my chair
Because I received a letter from Somewhere
In fact, it was from the Mayor of that town
Where the wind always makes a fearsome sound

Somewhere's Mayor Bryce appealed to me
To come and try my luck
By building up the town of Particular
He wrote to me to drive there in my truck

And that's the truth about how I arrived
Beneath a white cloud lenticular
I drove there to make sure
There'd be something in Particular!

Beneath that cloud lenticular
I stared up wondering, quite perplexed
About nothing in Particular
And then came thunder, I was hexed

Yes, it thundered in Particular
A small town on a plain
And since there was nothing in Particular
No one was troubled by the rain

But by then in Particular there was I
And along came my sons and wife by and by
And in that whole place through and through
There was absolutely nothing to do

NOTHING IN PARTICULAR

My children were not happy
That we'd come to make a life
In a place so barren
And neither was my wife

Her name is Sadie Hopkins
And you could tell by her stare
That rather than live in Particular
She'd have chosen Anywhere

But Anywhere
Is a town to the west
It's west of Somewhere
At the top of a crest

With help from my two sons
Named Joe and Jake
I set out to prove that life there
Would not be a mistake

I was as determined
As a man could be
That the town would grow large
As far as the eye could see

And so we decided
To build a general store
But so as not to be too general
We decided to sell much more

Yes, we stocked more than most
General stores would store
Our store was not small
Ten rooms and ceilings tall

And in all that we stocked
We sought variety
And as a result
Folks stopped by for tea

We built a restaurant
Right in the middle of our store
Lots of folks came from Somewhere
To see what our store was for

Folks came from Anywhere too
Because our store was new
Our store was more than it seemed
With more than anyone dreamed

"Until now," said Mayor Bryce,
"There's been nothing here at all
But now certainly
Lots of people will come to call"

He looked around, quite impressed
At all we had in store
And then he glanced in another room
Said he: "There's more!?"

Well, yes there was more
If you went through the next door
Where we kept the chandeliers
And stacked the mirrors, forty-four

And the bowls of crystals
Beside our tiger who never roared
A pet tiger named Homer
A tiger who was never bored

On the highest shelf in that room
We kept many toys
Toys including cars and trucks
Especially for the boys

Models they were with great detail
And all so very shiny
Some were impressively large
But most were rather tiny

NOTHING IN PARTICULAR

What we sold was for both
The young and the old
Lots of costumes
If the truth be told

Clothes of the past
And for the future too
Masks and boots and wigs
Quite a few

And vases with flowers
That always stayed fresh
And nets to catch sharks
Nets with wire mesh

Cages for wolves
And big brooms to sweep
All the cobwebs of the spiders
That do creep and creep

Milk bottles quite large
Made of plastic or glass
Republican elephants
And the Democrats' jackass

A whole room full of buttons
Of every color and size
A cupboard with flour
That will make your cakes rise

Old silent movies
On films made of nitrate
Extra ice for your pond
Where you can skate

Books of games
And jokes and riddles
Musical instruments
Lots of fiddles

Paul Jeffrey Davids

We sold practical things
That ordinary folks need
Potions and remedies
And band-aids if you bleed

Shrubs and bushes
And even trumpet vines
Trees for your forest
We specialize in large pines

Our sons who are handy
With tools of every kind
Make very big ladders
For use by the blind

Ladders that go clear
Up to the ceiling
And carrot peelers for carrots
That are in need of peeling

We sell can openers and unopened cans
Full of soups, vegetables and tasty jams
We sell muzzles for dogs and coyotes and lambs
And elk antlers and bull horns and horns from rams

There are quality telescopes
For looking at the moon
Scooters with engines
To get you places soon

Snowboards and surfboards
In case you get bored
And old model airplanes
That once really soared

We have carnival tents
And even a high wire
We carry six foot tall candles
That make quite a fire

NOTHING IN PARTICULAR

Saddles for horses
And even elephants too
Big pots for cannibals
For preparing their stew

Lanterns that flicker
Parrots that bite
Grass-chewing llamas
They are quite a sight

The bags of gold
Are not for sale
But the vegetables are
We have lots of kale

There's an old stamp collection
With ten thousand stamps
And pup tents and sleeping bags
For using in camps

We have typewriters that work
And computers that don't
We have turtles that walk
And some that won't

There are school books aplenty
With notes and scribbles
And a lifelike baby doll
That wets, spits and dribbles

We have several old cars
That were called horseless carriage
We have wedding dresses
And certificates for marriage

We have treadmills
For people who like to walk
We have microphones
For people who like to talk

Paul Jeffrey Davids

We have top hats and rabbits
If you're a magician
We have weight loss videos
If you're a dietician

Toy rockets ships
If you dream of visiting Mars
Flying saucer models
For pretend visits to stars

If it's your birthday
We can sell you a cake
And if your car won't stop
We'll sell you a brake

Political banners
And election bumper stickers
Remote controls of all types
Those things we call clickers

If you swim in a pool
We can provide flippers
Need chocolate sauce?
We have sauce dippers

For your next airplane trip
Here's a parachute
If you're joining an orchestra
Here's a good flute

A leash for your lion
A sweater for your dog
A nice cage for your hamster
A pond for your frog

Is there anything at all
That we did forget?
If you don't have a cat
Here's a cat you can pet

NOTHING IN PARTICULAR

We have practical things
For practical folks
If it's cigars you favor
We've got lots of smokes

If you sail the ocean
Well then here's a sail
Do you need a new boat?
Ours never fail

If you have neighbors
On them you can spy
Because we'll sell you binoculars
And here's why:
You never know
If they're coming or going
Now you'll see whatever
Through their window is showing

Our general store
Has ocean-faring items specific
Some for the Atlantic
And some for the Pacific

"Oh my," said Mayor Bryce
"Never have I seen
So many choices
It even makes me dream
Of places I've never been
And things I've never done
My friends, you sell everything
Under the sun"

Well, now folks did see
And everyone did know
Our potential for making
The town grow and grow

There was nothing in Particular
When we did arrive
The town was a dead place
But now it's alive

And word of our store
Has spread far and wide
People drive by and stare
And then they come inside

With folks leaving New York
And moving nearby
We needed a schoolhouse
I cannot lie

And we needed more houses
So soon they were built
A builder came from Scotland
Wearing a kilt

The hospital went up
And then the train station
Our town of Particular
Became a sensation

A locale where once
There was nothing at all
Had become a place
Where folks dropped by to call

Folks from the east
And folks from the west
With kids well behaved
But sometimes a pest
Who would tug on Mom's dress
And say it's a bore
Except for that super cool
General store

NOTHING IN PARTICULAR

My family is now fine here
My sons are all right
In our general store
They found a big kite

They're flying it up
To a cloud quite lenticular
While feeling mighty fine
About this town named Particular

So the next time you hear
Some blind people say
"There's nothing in Particular
Let's go on our way"
Please set them straight
Please set things right
Tell them if they could see
They'd see quite a sight

Because there's something in Particular
Yes, something quite nice
And to claim something different
You'll get a fight from Mayor Bryce

17. YOU'RE HERE, YOU'RE THERE

You're here, you're there
Why should I care?
Where you go
I do not know

You're here, you're there
You're in my hair
You are a pain
My heart you sprain

You come, you go
You leave, you blow
You run, you walk
You smirk, you talk

You do bother
Everyone you meet
Whether in a shop
Or on the street

You bug them, annoy them
And distract them too
They'd do anything at all
To get rid of you

But that's not true,
You're really quite cool
It's all my fault
I've been such a fool

I need you and love you
And want to hug you
It's always nice weather
When we're together

YOU'RE HERE, YOU'RE THERE

I'm head over heels
I'm as thrilled as can be
I jump up and down
I feel so free

I've got the shakes
I'm trembling and scared
For all of my life
I wish we were paired

Married's the word
That's what I seek
The problem is
I'm much too meek

I cannot even say hello
Or tell you my name
I cannot even raise a smile
To you I must seem lame

So I will now forget you
And never think of you again
I wish that you would run away
Right now! Don't ask me when!

You're here, you're there
Why should I care?
Where you go
I do not know

You're here, you're there
You're in my hair
You are a pain
My heart you sprain

But I love you so
That's the truth, you know
Please never leave me
Please never go

18. MY LIFE AS A POET

If I could go back in time
While floating on this very rhyme
And choose a new profession
Here is my sincere confession
A judge I certainly would not be
I'd probably set the wrong guys free
Male model? – No, I'm not a stud
Doctor? I can't stand the sight of blood
Traffic cop? – My arms get tired fast
Data processor? – My eyes would never last
Pilot? – Not with my great fear of heights
Ballet dancer? I will never wear tights
Lawyer? You'd have to read me my rights
Boxer? No – I'm allergic to fights
Sailor? I get seasick from the waves
Coal miner? It's much too dark in caves
Facebook friend? That makes no money
Comedian? I'm rarely funny
Politician? I'd scare away the votes
Navy captain? – You know what I think of boats
Carpenter – well, I have ten thumbs
Deadbeat? I'd never join the bums
Some people think I'm much too inflexible
But another profession for me? It's just not textable
But writing poems – that's not too tough
Thinking in rhyme? Well that's not rough
So if I could go back in time
While floating on this very rhyme
Choose a new profession – I couldn't
Live another life? I wouldn't

19. YOU'RE GOOD, YOU'RE BAD

You're good, oh yes
You are so good
You're always on time
You are sublime

You do no wrong
Can this last for long?
Oh I do hope so
You're incredibly fine

Upstanding with morals
You'll stand on your laurels
Your principals I cherish
It's you that I relish

You would never permit becoming a flit
A wormy crum-bum so foul
You'd never dare give off a terrible stink
Or make the fine folk howl

It's because you're courageous and fine
You'd never turn on a dime
Nor ever commit any crime
Nor in the pen do any time

You're the pride of our life
And we like your wife
You're so good, oh you're good
Like fine wine

But what happened? Oh no!
Your bad side you did show
You've shocked us
And let us down so

Paul Jeffrey Davids

It's like you've gone mad
Our tolerance has grown thin
We know that you're bad
And we can't win

A bad example you are
The worst by far
You are no doll
You are no dove

For with all your might
You'll put up a fight
Against charity and mercy
And love

Oh, you're bad, you are so bad
Don't you know you can't join our team?
Because you're so evil, a genuine devil
And worse even than that – you're mean!

Oh my what you'll do
When they're not watching you!
It's disgusting, insulting and worse
You're foul and so evil
You'll cause such an upheaval
That I think this poem should be terse
Because the bad that you do
Shall far out-live you
And this world you do make much worse
Yes, I think this poem should be terse

But can that be true
Because the good that you do
Far outweighs all the rest
We suspect that you're good
Because you're so good
So we'll put you to a test

YOU'RE GOOD, YOU'RE BAD

You're good, you're good
Oh yes, you are so good
You're on time, you're so fine
You're sublime

You can do no wrong
Can this last for long?
Oh I hope so
You're incredibly fine

20. YOU ARE A GIRL, A BOY AM I

You are a girl
A boy am I
A girl you are
I will not lie

The girl is you
The boy is me
On that we certainly
Can agree

We're not the same
You're such a pain
You are so serious
But life's a game

You are so wrong
To hate my song
It's not so long
And you are wrong

I made it up
To bring good luck
Don't run away
I want to play

Yes, I run and play
And I sing all day
You always sleep
Are you so weak?

Wake up, I say
It is the day
I'll sleep, you say
Go away

YOU ARE A GIRL, A BOY AM I

I draw and paint
I never faint
My life you taint
You are no saint

You hide and run
You are no fun
Now here's the key
Come play with me

While I make hay
You run away
You will not play
I'll make you pay

You are so swell
You're feeling well
A boy am I
I'll kiss and tell

I am not coy
I'm just a boy
I've got a toy
I am a boy

You've things to do
I say poo-poo
You're in a whirl
You are a girl

Come play with me
And you will see
It's fun to play
And climb a tree

I'm full of joy
I'm never coy
You I do annoy
Because I'm a boy

You have a dress
It will unfurl
You show it off
You are a girl

I like your hair
I'll sit and stare
Can we be friends?
Let's make amends

It's you and me
We are not three
Let's have some fun
Come play with me

I think of you
You think of me
We are just two
We are not three

You are a girl
A boy am I
A girl you are
I will not lie

21. ELENA'S JOURNEY

One thing is sure
Here's a fantasy pure
It sprang from my mind
In record time

It is the story of a girl
A girl quite young
Her name I have
On the tip of my tongue

To begin the tale
I must remember her name
And if I've forgotten
Then I'm to blame

Oh yes, Elena she is
A girl of such imagination
Elena lived far away
Not in any known nation

In fact, Elena lived
On a world very far
From our world the Earth
She lived near another Star

Far from our sun
Across the Milky Way
That was where Elena lived
The world where she did play

Elena loved her mother
And Mother's stories about our world
Earth was such a mixed-up place
Thought Elena as she twirled

The Earth was not a real place
Her mother often said
It was just a land from storybooks
A world some people dread

Because they have wars
And they chop all the trees down
And the birds have all flown away
And there's smoke above the towns

And the fish have all been scooped up
And of horses there are few
And all the ice melts on the mountaintops
What will those people do?

Elena tired of such tales
Of that planet named Earth
She preferred her own world
Which is called the planet Chirp

For chirping is what birds like to do
When they all begin to sing
And singing is a wonderful thing
It has a very soothing ring

Also it is soothing
To be an artist who paints
Elena's paintings were so beautiful
They almost made people faint

They had colors galore
And wonderful swirls
And showed splendid towns
Full of little girls

Life was perfect for Elena
Until the day she could not find
The birthday box from her mother
With its magical comb inside

ELENA'S JOURNEY

So Elena lost her magical comb
Where in Chirp did it go?
It had vanished from sight
So her hair it did grow

Elena's hair grew very long
Passed her shoulders wide
And all the way down her back
Her hair did glide

It reached her legs
And then her feet
Her hair was very long
And never neat

A brush she found
Her hair was tangled
The brush did not work
She felt so jangled

A pair of scissors
Could help her so
If she cut her hair
But no, no, no!

Her hair was so long
It was difficult to measure
But she never cut her hair
It brought her so much pleasure

One day she had some cookies
And she drank some tea
And she packed a little bag
And then she went off to sea

She sailed the North Sea
The ocean vast
And then she remembered
Her splendid past

She thought of her dear mother
Whom she did love
Her mother had a ladybird
A beautiful white dove

In the sky the dove had found
A kingdom of light
With glowing towers
Such a marvelous sight

The dove told her secrets
That it did whisper
In melodious chirps
So Elena kissed her

As she sailed o'er the waves
Of the tumbling sea
Elena thought of all
She wished to be

A princess or queen
Or a duchess quite fair
And always she'd keep
Her very long hair

A doctor or lawyer
Or a mathematician keen
A scientist brilliant
Or a model so lean

A race car driver
Or jockey atop a horse
She'd win every race
Of course

As the waves grew larger
She had many visions
She would write long poems
With no revisions

ELENA'S JOURNEY

The waves were so high
She could reach them and touch
The tips of those waves
Now they were rough

The boat pitched and tumbled
The sky grew dark
A bird approached
It was a lark

And then soon after
Just above
Came her mother's bird
That splendid dove

The birds did chatter
Of storms quite fierce
Her peace was shattered
Her dreams now pierced

A voyage at sea
Was all very nice
With tranquil waters
All sugar and spice

But if the boat did lurch
And water hit the deck
Her hair would get wet
She would need a hair net

But of hair nets there were none
And no towels for drying
And her toes were now damp
She almost started crying

She went to her cabin
And plotted to depart
By drawing a picture
She stepped into her art

Paul Jeffrey Davids

It was a picture of the kingdom
The kingdom of light
Oh, so high in the sky
By day and by night

At night it did glow
With stars everywhere
At those twinkling night stars
She decided to stare

She found one star to visit
But it was so far
She couldn't sail there
Or go in a car

And how to fly there
When she had no wings?
Then the lark and the dove
Both began to sing

They sang of great joy
That came from a wish
Like ice cream or pudding
Served in a dish

So she wished and she prayed
To fly to that star
And fly there she did
No matter how far

The star had nine planets
Elena chose one
The green world with oceans
Third one from the sun

It looked like the Earth
But was the Earth real?
Wasn't Earth just a fantasy
Made up for little girls?

ELENA'S JOURNEY

The sky it was cloudy
With clouds white and puffed
They seemed full of cotton
With which they were stuffed

She set down on a cloud
But just for a rest
A hawk rather nearby
Proved to be quite a pest

It squawked and it squabbled
And flapped its wings wide
Elena did not understand
Its warning implied
That all was not well
On the world down below
Rivers were saddened
They were losing their flow

Mountains were sweating
From the harsh heat
Their ice-caps were melting
And wheat fields had no wheat

Something foul was afoot
On that planet, the hawk cried
Elena jumped off the cloud
And that's when she spied
A jungle below her
With the tallest of trees
When she landed, a flower told her
We now have no bees!

Flowers needed bees
To distribute their pollen
Without them, then no flowers
And the trees they had fallen

Not fallen, oh no
At their trunks they were cut
Sliced by machines
And then barked a mutt

The dog it was snappy
And it jumped a lot too
Messing up Elena's hair
What was she to do?

She tried to run
But then she fell down
Her hair was all matted
Where was there a town?

A town she soon found
With the help of a mouse
The mouse it soon led her
To the Mayor's house

The Mayor was fretful
And so frightened too
"Oh tell me, Elena," he said
"What am I to do?
Machines cut our forests
And the trees they do fall
And now there's no honey
And there's much smoke in the fall
The men burn up the trees
Soon there will be no trees at all
And there's no ice in the mountains
So let's put in a call
To New York where the nations
In a tall building do meet
To try to solve the world's problems
That would prove quite a feat"

ELENA'S JOURNEY

The phone call went through
The other voice it did plead
"Please come to the United Nations
In our hour of need"

How to get to New York?
The Mayor did worry
In the jungle there were no planes
To get there in a hurry

But another bird arrived
This one was a stork
"Climb onto my back," he squawked
"And we'll fly to New York"

"Now just a minute," Elena cried
Checking the watch on her wrist
"How is it possible I'm on the Earth
When the Earth does not exist?
How is it possible I've come so far
To a place that's upside-down
To a world where happiness is rare
And sensible people can't be found?
Why would I choose to come to Earth
When trillions of planets there are?
I want to go back to Chirp
Even though it is far"

The Mayor told Elena
To climb onto the stork
Otherwise they would fail
Ever to reach New York

So the Mayor and Elena
Leaped onto the stork
The Mayor brought lunch
With even two forks

But as fly onward they did
Through the clouds suddenly tore
A missile quite dreadful
Down below a great war!

The stork took a tumble
And to the ground they did fall
There were armies around them
With soldiers all so tall

Those soldiers attacked
With weapons advanced
Then a white horse rode by
He leaped and he pranced

To safety the horse took them
Elena, The Mayor and the stork
They defended themselves
With those very sharp forks

At a pond they dismounted
And they heard from a frog
That the pond was now fading
Turned into a bog

Once fish had all swum there
In schools very large
But men scooped them all up
Using a barge

The horse and stork felt sorrow
For the pond with no fish
The horse neighed and whispered
As he declared a great wish

A world such as this one
Had become a sad world of course
And with so many wars
Soon not even a horse

ELENA'S JOURNEY

Not one horse at all
Would gallop across this land
And the gardens and forests
Would all turn to sand

"What a world this is!"
Elena exclaimed
"Such a world without horses
Wild or tamed!"

Atop the flying stork
They again took up their stations
And soon Elena spoke
At the United Nations

"Oh, people of Earth,
You have so much to learn,"
Elena spoke plainly
In a voice very firm
"Your planet has problems
More than just a few
I'll teach you of my world
I have lessons for you
I am sure I can show you
How to set things right
How to love one another
And don't pick fight after fight
Don't foul up your air
With your chimneys and the car
You burn up the rain forests
Is this who you are?"

She told them she'd come
From a world very far
That she'd arrived at their Earth
By wishing on a star

In her world there was peace
For birds, horses and frogs
And the fish in the waters
Whether oceans or bogs

In her world were no wars
No weapons at all
People let the trees live
No matter how tall

"Lay down your weapons,"
said Elena in a voice stern
"No more fighting among men
And no trees must burn
Respect your planet
And it will respect you back
Nurture feelings of fellowship
For such feelings you lack"

Her words so wise
Made some nations mad
They insisted she leave
And when she left they were glad

But she had no friends
In that big city New York
She looked for a bottle
That was plugged with a cork

When the bottle she found
She pulled off the cork
"There's a ship in that bottle!"
She exclaimed to the stork

That ship was her vessel
Which had come from afar
To take her home
To her distant star

But small it now was
Too small to sail
At her present size
This was all bound to fail

And then it did rain
It even started to hail
The hail cracked the bottle
The ship fell into a pail

The pail grew quite large
And the ship it grew too
"Come back on board!"
Shouted someone she knew

It was her mother
On her shoulder, the dove
What a wonderful time
To see someone she loved

Mother helped her aboard
Her mother so smart
On the boat was her cabin
Filled with her art

Her paintings large
And her small ones too
Every morning and evening
She painted anew

Paintings of the universe
Swirling and whirling
Paintings with edges
That kept curling and curling

Just like her hair
When it was all dry
But thinking about her hair
Made her want to cry

Mother scolded Elena
For sailing the North Sea
She had no permission at all
A sailor to be

"But mother, I've discovered,
A planet once green
And now life there
Is not at all what it seems
A planet with history
From centuries passed
Great towns and cities
I have questions unasked
But the people of Earth
They quarrel and fight
They need someone like me
To set their world right"

Her mother reminded her
She was still a child
With hair much too long
For a journey this wild

Elena painted a new picture
Of the kingdom of light
With the huge glowing towers
It all looked just right

So into that picture
They sailed their great ship
The boat toppled and tumbled
And then it did tip

Elena was falling
And her mother too
Onto a crystal tower
All covered with dew

ELENA'S JOURNEY

The morning's soft rain
It was a light drizzle
And Elena's long hair
The dew caused to frizzle

Twinkling lights sent wisdom
Throughout crystal towers
The morning's rain
Turned into strong showers

"Oh Mother, if only Earth
Could learn the lessons I taught
Then their planet would not perish
Nor would they be fraught"

Said her mother: "Planets are many
So many trillions
Millions of perfect ones
But troubled ones, billions
Yes, planets are many
And wise lessons are rare
Instead of worrying about lessons
Let's tend to your hair!"

Said Elena: "I've tried, yes really
My hair to brush
But my hair is so tangled
The brush it does crush"

Her mother did calm her
Revealing a box of stone
For inside that box
Was the magical comb

With that comb she untangled
Elena's jangled hair
With that comb she soon straightened
Elena's hair so fair

Paul Jeffrey Davids

From the kingdom of light
They then leaped through the sky
Falling onto soft mattresses
Never knowing why

"Oh goodness," said Elena
"I'm at home in my bed
I fell asleep quickly
While that story you read
That story about Earth
The planet far away
That has such troubles
Yesterday and always"

"Go to sleep, Elena,"
Her mother did say
"Tomorrow's another day
And then you can play
But no more shall I read you
Fairy stories about Earth
An imaginary planet
That has so little mirth
A planet whose troubles
Are more than a few
An old, tired planet
That once was so new
Back in the days of perfection
When every imaginable confection
Existed on that world so pure
It was a planet needing no cure
A planet of the forest and plain
Singing every refrain
With rivers and streams
Pure as sweet dreams"

22. YOU'RE UP, YOU'RE DOWN

You're the luckiest person
Who ever will live
Happiness and luck
Are all yours to give

A wink and a smile
You are all aglow
My, you've really got
All your ducks in a row

You are so up
You're soaring in space
You're a perfect person
Just look at your face

How did you get here
To a state so sublime
The world is your oyster
You're a master of time

You're up, you're up
Boy, are you ever up,
You're higher than the sky
And you don't even try

You've got it made
Totally made in the shade
And you're always employed
You always get paid

But oh no, what is this?
What can be the matter?
Your perfect comportment
Has begun to shatter

Now you sleep late every day
Works gets in the way
You are bothered by something
You want to do nothing

Suddenly nothing goes right
You can't put up a fight
You feel there's a bitter end
And bad vibrations you send

Why the big change?
What's come over you, pray tell?
You look terrible now
All shot to hell

You're tired and flabby
And weak, a disgrace
Have you given up
On the whole human race?

You've come unglued
You're regularly booed
Life was fine and dandy
Sweeter than candy

But you can't even remember
Having one happy day
You hate the world
But you won't dare say

Your pain is your own
Private Hades and hell
Oh, from great heights
You tumbled and fell

You're down, my friend
We can't even find you
You'll drown you're so down
Please don't take your friends too

YOU'RE UP, YOU'RE DOWN

There must be some hope
To put an end to that frown
You're down and washed up
So washed up, you're washed down

Perhaps a new friend
Will now wend his way
Into your heart
Coaxing you to stay
Afloat on the boat
And in a mood so brave
You'll recapture life
And good spirits you'll save

We hope so, we do
We hope and we pray
For to lose you to sadness
We don't herald that day

For you are the one
Who gave us all hope
You are our friend
Please stay on the boat

23. WE'RE MOVING, WE'RE STAYING

(*Note to the Reader:* In 2011, my wife and I had some challenging moments. For several years she had been working with an architect to plan how to redesign our house to remodel the kitchen entirely in our California bungalow home. The new kitchen would absorb the back porch and side porch for more space, add a skylight and every modern feature any woman — or man – could want for a kitchen. The questions were: could we afford it? And how stressful would construction prove to be? Would it make more sense to move to a larger house that already had a fine kitchen? That predicament was the inspiration for this poem.)

You want a new kitchen
Because you love to cook
And you know I love food
I'm overweight – look

But please starve me, I say
Feed me no more
A new kitchen, you say
With a brand new floor

You plan your new kitchen
Then I see the bill
The money they want
It's over the hill

So I get an idea
Let's move out of this place
Let's get a new home
With a kitchen that's great

Let's buy a new house
Yeah, that would be nice
You like that idea
So we check out the price

WE'RE MOVING, WE'RE STAYING

No deals to be had
These prices hurt so
We'd end up flat broke
We don't have the dough

To get a great place
It's a million or more
I don't want more debt
Because I know the score

I say: "Honey, let's not budge
And I'm not being funny"
You say: "We'll keep looking
And we'll manage the money"

So we're moving, we're moving
We're going, let's go
We shoot for the moon
But the moon just won't glow

I say no to the short sales
All the kitchens are small
And the foreclosures we see
Make us both want to stall

But you want more space
So we search and we search
Then the banks and the sellers
Leave us in the lurch

"Darling, let's rethink this thing
Let's reverse gears somehow
Let's just stay where we are
But not remodel – not now
Because we've always lived here
And right here we'll dwell
But if we remodel the kitchen
Life will be hell"

You say, "If you want to stay here
A new kitchen's a must
A non-negotiable demand
And my instincts you'll trust"

I look again at those plans
For that new kitchen with no rust
Great plans for a boom
But not for a bust

You say: "The kitchen this year
Listen well, I insist"
And you put your foot down
Well, I could not resist

I did see the light
A new kitchen would cost less
Than buying a new house
But life would be a mess
For four to six months
With the hammers and saws
Noise night and day
With hardly a pause

Once the decision was made
To the occasion we both rose
We ate out for six months
On my waistline it shows

The new kitchen we've been building
The new kitchen we'll take
And now I'll admit
It was no mistake

The cabinets and new floors
Fine buffets and new doors
The great windows for light
Why did we ever fight?

WE'RE MOVING, WE'RE STAYING

Cupboards and skylight
Even TV and surround-sound
Clean walls and great pantry
The best all around

Granite countertops
And each brand new appliance
Great sinks and disposals
I abandon defiance

It's utterly splendid
So how can I grouse?
But we spent more for the kitchen
Than we spent for the house!

24. YOU'VE WON, YOU'VE LOST

(*Note to the Reader:* At the beginning of my career as a television producer, I worked for F. Lee Bailey, the famous attorney. I was a segment producer on LIE DETECTOR, his syndicated television show. One of the cases was so unusual, I never forgot it. A lottery winner in Pennsylvania was declared, and then instead of being paid, he was quickly arrested. The claim of the authorities was that he had five of the six numbers right on his lottery ticket, and he had decided to commit the crime of changing the sixth number – thinking he could easily change a six to an eight. He was caught. That case became the inspiration for this poem.)

You're the best by far
You've nothing to fear
You guessed all the numbers
No one else came near

The lottery's tough and nobody does it
With five numbers plus bonus to boot
You are just the greatest, you now are our hero
For you we always shall root

One chance in a billion, no make it a trillion
To come out on top like that
To you, my dear sir, what can I do?
I shall offer to tip my hat

Ninety million you've won – by George, what fun!
You shall spend and spend till you drop
You are made for life, so find a good wife
You're sure to come out on top

But what's this, oh no
Please say it's not true
Whatever has fate
Just done to you?

YOU'VE WON, YOU'VE LOST

Those numbers you have
All six in a row
We thought they had made you
But now you're laid low

One of them's wrong
Your eight is a six
You changed it, you liar
You're in such a fix!

You can't change the numbers
To make them just right
They've canceled your party
So fade into the night

You'll find out what happens
When you do lie
You said you had won
But now you will cry

The lottery's sacred
And the sweepstakes too
You lost fair and square
What will happen to you?

The cops they are coming
To take you away
You falsified and lied
And now you shall pay

You said you had won
But you lost fair and square
Your fall has been swift
But why should I care?

Good riddance, they say
For you tried to cheat
You said you won
But you sir were beat

25. WE LOVE YOU, WE HATE YOU

(*Note to the Reader:* Have you ever felt "in" one minute and "out" the next, only to be invited back "in" but probably for some ulterior motive? Think of some famous actors and singers. One minute loved and admired, the next minute cast out and hated. Then loved again. Then hated. Then loved. That has happened with many entertainment celebrities. And politicians. It even happens in ordinary families! That observation was my inspiration. This is the only poem in this book that is non-rhyming. It is free verse that came to me very spontaneously. I recorded it as a song in Nashville and you can find it on the Internet. Perhaps there's more passion that comes out in the song than on the page, but you'll get the idea, especially if this has happened to you!)

We love you
We love you
We love you
We love you
Oh no we don't!
We hate you!

We hate you
We hate you
We hate you
We hate you
Oh no that's all wrong!
We love you!

We love you
We love you
We need you
Oh, how we need you
But no that's not right
We hate you!

WE LOVE YOU, WE HATE YOU

No, we love you
Indeed we love you
Please come back
We so need you!

Did we hurt your feelings?
Oh no, we didn't mean it
We just can't go on
Without you

But how can we love you
When we really hate you?
Get out of here
We hate you!

Hate you,
Detest you
Despise you
You stink

Don't grace our sight again
Get the hell out of here
Don't you come back again
Go!

But you're so dear
Be near!
We need you!
Oh, how we need you!

We love you so much
Because you're great!
Your talent!
It's amazing!
You're incredible!
Come back!
We love you
Yes, we need you!

But excuse me
What did we say?
How could we get it so wrong?
We hate you!

We hate you
We hate you
Get the hell out of here
And don't ever come back!

But we didn't mean it
We really care
Your talent – it takes awhile
For us to build up an appreciation for it
To get to the very heart of it
We didn't understand you at first
But now! We see!
You're worth a fortune to us
Our whole company
Our whole future
How can we ever go on without you?

But we'll try
Somehow we'll try to survive
With you gone
Forever
Did you hear us?
Get the hell out of here!
We hate you
We hate you!!
We despise you
We detest you!!

But really
When the truth be told—
We love you
We love you
Oh yes, we really do
LOVE YOU!

26. PROFESSOR HACK HARDDRIVE'S™ WIKILEAKS POEM

(*Note to the Reader:* Professor Hack HardDrive is a sympathetic but villainous character I created. There are many villains who have won their way into our hearts. Some people are born to be bad, and they are incomprehensible. However, Professor Hack HardDrive is evil in a way that we can understand, because his schemes and crimes are specific to our modern, technological era. Forty years ago there were no hard drives to hack, and identity theft was not yet a common crime. Professor Hack HardDrive uses technology to get his way and cause trouble. I have so far recorded three of the Professor Hack HardDrive poems as rap songs, and below you'll find a picture of him that I painted for a CD cover.)

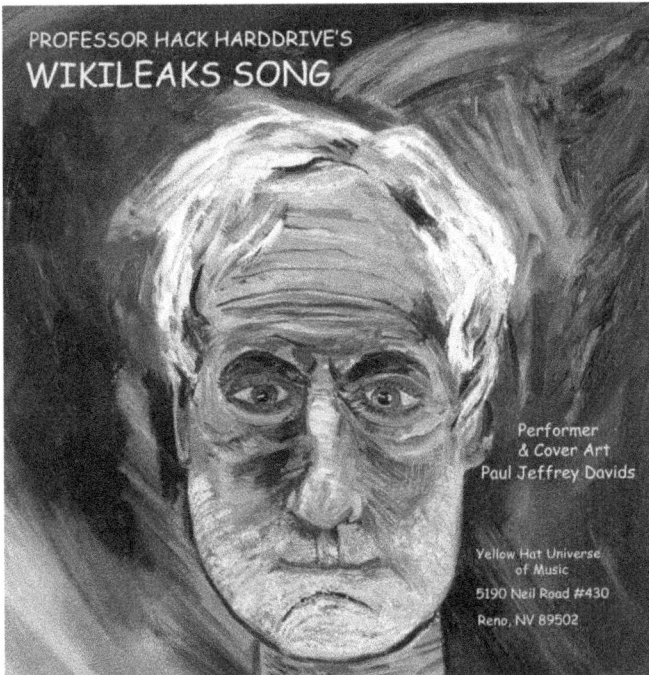

PROFESSOR HACK HARDDRIVE'S
WIKILEAKS SONG

Performer
& Cover Art
Paul Jeffrey Davids

Yellow Hat Universe
of Music
5190 Neil Road #430
Reno, NV 89502

Paul Jeffrey Davids

I'm Professor Hack HardDrive
And now I'm all locked up
They threw me in jail
They think I'm clean out of luck

I hacked the wrong hard drive
And the files that I took
Are all filled with secrets
Come on -- have a look!

The Pentagon has put me
On their most dangerous list
They say I'm a threat to national security
They call me terrorist

Don't think that I'm crazy
My mind is still sound
I didn't put them on Google
All those secrets that I found

I downloaded them all
On a thumb drive real small
I'm gonna make big trouble
Wickileaks I'm gonna call

In my cell I've got a cell phone
With Internet access and all
Let them find another patsy
I'm not takin' the fall

Hey Julian, my friend
You're on a very tough road
But I've got two million secrets
Ready for you to upload

PROFESSOR HACK HARDDRIVE'S ™ WIKILEAKS POEM

UFO's and chem trails
And lots of voter fraud, too
Fukushima and plutonium
Now San Onofre is through

Enron, they've got the bomb
Do not wait, detonate
CIA controls your mind
Columbine is not so fine

911 implosion
Nothing's as it seems
Conspiracies are not fads
This world's just full of bad dreams

Waco is wacko
And Oklahoma City's dead
It all started with JFK
A bullet in the head

Then along came Bobby Kennedy
And then they shot Martin Luther King dead
"I am not a crook," Nixon said
Oh, all the lies that guy fed

OJ is not okay
Aspartame is deadly
USA is going bankrupt
Bilderberger is the medley

Chads are hangin' everywhere
Are they gonna parole Manson?
Angels don't play this HAARP
It's a military ransom

Three Mile Island, Chernobyl
DDT and so much more
Terrorists are gonna get the bomb
We're all at death's very door

99

Armageddon and Nibiru
It's 2012 – oh, Uncle Sam!
Area 51 has aliens!
Government is a sham

Acid rain will rot your brain
Smog will fry your noodle
Hybrid foods will poison you
Thanks to Yankee Doodle

The Masons worship Isis
There are flying saucers on the moon!
Lordy, get me out of this place
And make it very, very soon!

Oh Julian, please spread the word
From Wikileaks please leak
All these secrets I did hack
You're awake, come on – take a peak!

I'm Professor Hack HardDrive
And I may be a little bit whacked
But I've been jailed, I did get nailed
So I'm uploading all the stuff I hacked!

I'm Professor Hack HardDrive!
Yeah!

27. PROFESSOR HACK HARDDRIVE'S™ ELECTION POEM

I'm Professor Hack HardDrive
And I stand for honesty
Elections should be fair and square
And should always elect ME

I'm just joking, okay?
Don't be so serious
And if your guy doesn't win
Don't get so furious

You win some, you lose some
And if you're not on my side
You'll lose more than you win
I've got God on my side

But more than God,
A secret weapon have I
It's a special satellite
Way up there in the sky

When I want to change the votes
To make them come out right
I send a few quick signals
To that satellite out of sight

Like a professional gambler
Fixing cards without detection
I shuffle the votes
And fix the election

I have no conscience at all
No pangs of remorse
Because the best man always wins
And he's always *my* man, of course

Take a few votes from Peter
And give them to Paul
The fraud is invisible
And victory margin quite small

Don't call me a criminal
Or dastardly liar
All elections, you know
Come right down to the wire

If I didn't play favorites
To make the best guy win
Our elected officials
Would be knee-deep in sin

Fixing elections
Is like medicine for the soul
If the bums win the office
It will take a tough toll

So I always make sure
That the best guy is on top
And the best guy is *my* guy
And your guy I'll stop

I just hack a few hard drives
At a few polling places
You should see the expressions
On everyone's faces

My country I save
From a terrible fate
By tossing the bad guys
The ones that I hate

The fact that you like
The candidates that lose
Is not my problem
Please pass me some booze

PROFESSOR HACK HARDDRIVE'S™ ELECTION POEM

Let's all celebrate
That I choose who prevails
If I don't do that
Then our government fails

So thank me you must
And bless me you will
Because if my guy loses
Then the winner I'll have to kill

Just kidding, of course
Hey, c'mon – *just kidding!*
Of course!

I'm Hack
Hack HardDrive
Make that Professor –- to you – Hack HardDrive
Yeah!

28. PROFESSOR HACK HARDDRIVE'S™ IDENTITY THEFT POEM

For protection and justice
You'll parade and you'll lobby
But identity theft
Has become my main hobby

I'm Professor Hack HardDrive
And I'm going to hack
All your deepest secrets
And then you will lack
Everything that you cherish
And I'll never give back
Your personal identify
No, you'll never get it back

Your social security number
That's where I'll start
And then on to your bank accounts
Like stealing your heart

Your driver's license
That's the number I crave
And then there's your passport
And your photo, I'll save

In fact, I'll download
Every photo you conceal
In your secret files
Oh, this is unreal

I'll just snatch all those photos
That reveal all you hide
The porn that you lust for
I'm along for the ride

PROFESSOR HACK HARDDRIVE'S™ IDENTITY THEFT POEM

Your credit cards are just waiting
For me to inspect
I'll get all those numbers
And then I'll add to your debt

I'll take all your passcodes
And PayPal account
Your money will vanish
I'll wipe you clean out

Oh, for protection and justice
You'll parade and you'll lobby
But identity theft
Has become my main hobby

You'll beg and you'll plead
For me to leave you alone
But I'll wipe out who you are
Let's start with your cell phone!

That contact list of yours
All those numbers to call
I'll phone your whole list
And I'll blackmail them all

Your security box
It's so safe, you think
I'll pop it right open
Some call me a fink

You think you're so special
And powerful too
All your assets I'll grab
And then you'll be through

Oh yeah, for protection and justice
You'll parade and you'll lobby
But identity theft
Has become my main hobby

While I'm on the loose
You'll take it in the chin
Technology rules
You just can't win

I'm Professor Hack HardDrive
And I'll take it all
I'll shrink you to nothing
I'll make you so small

You probably hope
That I'll get thrown in the clink
And regret all I've done
Because my morals, they stink

Fat chance, I say
And lots of luck
Hey, can you spare me a dollar?
I sure need a buck

29. PROFESSOR HACK HARDDRIVE'S™ DOWNLOADING YOU

I'm Professor Hack HardDrive
Of the techno-geek kind
I'm a computer nerd
A little out of my mind

With you I'm infatuated
And I'm so exasperated
Obsessed to the max
So I'll send you a FAX
Because my email won't work
You must think I'm a jerk
But you're really so dear
Darling, it's you I need near

So I'm downloading you
Yes, I'm downloading YOU

My laptop's here
You've nothing to fear
They say it just tickles
As I download your pixels

With you in my laptop
I'll always have you
Try to escape me
You'll see what I do

Nine hundred gigabytes
That's what you are
Your brain and your fame
And your face, you're a star

So I'm downloading YOU
Yes, I'm downloading YOU

Paul Jeffrey Davids

I'm Professor Hack HardDrive
Of the techno-geek kind
I'm a computer nerd
A little out of my mind

I won't clone you, won't phone you
I won't be a pest
But with you in my laptop
Darling, I'll never rest

On Mondays and Thursdays
I'll clean up your file
On Tuesdays and Fridays
You'll de-frag for awhile

On Sundays and Wednesdays
I'll de-bug your hair
Holidays and Saturdays
You'll be my software

Because I'm downloading YOU
Yes, I'm downloading YOU

I'll love you to pieces
I'll love you to bits
Now you are my website
You'll get ten million hits
I'll greet you, I'll feed you
Sixty-four RAM
I'll bite all your megabytes
Because that's who I am

You won't catch a virus
You are in no danger
You're with Professor Hack HardDrive
There's nobody stranger

PROFESSOR HACK HARDDRIVE'S™ DOWNLOADING YOU

I'll email your photo
In a file I'll unzip
I'll back up all your data
On my microchip

Cause I'm downloading YOU, sweetheart
Yes, I'm downloading YOU

I'm Professor Hack HardDrive
Of the techno-geek kind
A computer nerd
A little out of my mind!

30. A WEE ONE WITH ALISTAIR MACLEAN

(*Note to the Reader:* What is a "wee one"? A drink, of course! "Let's have a wee one" means let's have a shot of vodka – or gin or whiskey! This poem is serious as well as humorous, and it is autobiographical. It is about a noted celebrity: the late Alistair MacLean, the best-selling author of action and suspense novels including THE GUNS OF NAVARONE. It is also about his agent, Paul Kohner, who was known as the Magician of Sunset Boulevard and who gave me my first full-time job in the entertainment business as a script-reader for his clients such as Charles Bronson, Max von Sydow and John Huston. The story takes place the week Alistair MacLean became a Kohner client, when a deal was made for Alistair to write a treatment for Columbia Pictures for his story, THE SEAWITCH. Until the advent of Stephen King, Alistair MacLean was the best-selling male author of all time, topped in his day only by a single female writer: Agatha Christie. Sales of his books were in the tens of millions. Some photos are included at the end of this poem of the people and events in the poetic tale. Below is a photo of Alistair MacLean.)

Alistair MacLean (1922 - 1987)

A WEE ONE WITH ALISTAIR MACLEAN

In the younger years of marriage
Life was not so hard
I worked for the Magician
Of Sunset Boulevard

Paul Kohner was his name
He filled me with wonder
A movie agent he was
With a reputation like thunder

His clients were many
They all had much fame
If I listed them here
You would know every name

An older gentleman was he
Inspiring beyond measure
That he gave me a job
Filled me with pleasure

Movie deals every day
In Hollywood, so many sales
And he thought that I had
A talent for tales

He called me script reader
And my salary was earned
Because with many scripts sent to him
To me he then turned

The year as I recall
Was nineteen seventy-six
And there were many stories
Paul Kohner asked me to fix

And then one day
A new writer Paul Kohner signed
THE GUNS OF NAVARONE was his book
In awe, how I sighed

Paul Jeffrey Davids

Alistair MacLean of Scotland
This remarkable new client
Among authors worldwide
An indisputable giant

VARIETY announced
The deal for his movie story new
It was called The SEAWITCH
It was to become a novel too
A story of an oil derrick
And hostages to be
A plan for a nuclear explosion
Not so far out at sea

To his office Paul Kohner called me
And sat me right down
"Young Paul" he then addressed me
"Alistair MacLean is now in town
I see from your report that you've read
H.M.S. ULYSSES
That was his very first book
And you say that it quite pleased
Alistair will appreciate
Your review so well written
But I'm afraid he must now chew
Much more than he's bitten
The SEAWITCH story
He must write in two weeks
But of unfortunate secrets
To you I must speak
Alistair has a weakness
For drinking Scotch on the run
Yes, whiskey could prove his downfall
Or from rum he could be undone
Bourbon too
Has its fierce way with him
And liqueur is a problem
And did I mention gin?"

A WEE ONE WITH ALISTAIR MACLEAN

Paul Kohner continued
His face fraught with worry
He told the next part slowly
Clearly in no hurry

"From a hospital near
We just obtained his release
His liver is toxic
And I have no peace
We have hired a nurse
To keep watch like a cop
If Alistair tries to drink
Then the drinking she'll stop
There are also two lads
Friends who do help him some
A diamond merchant and an artist
From Holland they've come
Alistair will surely like you
When he sees your review
But it's a spy that I need
And here's what you're to do"

The plan it was told to me
Some of it was quite coy
But in step one
I was just a delivery boy

I was to drive to Columbia Pictures
Where all hands were on deck
Alistair's advance was ten grand
I was to pick up his check

I was to take him the money
And make sure he was writing
And see that those Dutchmen
Were not fomenting in-fighting

Alistair needed no distractions
So he could finish his work
But my boss feared that the nurse
Might drive him berserk

She had promised no liquor
Would be found at the house
But having no whiskey
Alistair was expected to grouse

It was a solid black home
I knocked on his door
Holding the check in my hand
Hearing footsteps across the floor

First did I meet
Zeljko and Willem
Artist and diamond merchant
They invited me in

Said Willem: "Before you meet Alistair
Please sit down and remain still
Alistair is now resting
And brief you we will
It may sound like fiction
But we've never lied
This very black house
Is where Marilyn Monroe died
Alistair right now
Lies in Marilyn's bed
He's dreaming of her
But more must be said
Today he did injure
His forefingers each one
The two fingers he types with
He does not use his thumbs"

A WEE ONE WITH ALISTAIR MACLEAN

Willem did continue
With a glint in his eye
All this information I absorbed
But I was not trained as a spy

"Alistair never mastered
How to type with ten fingers
And the pain it impedes him
The pain that now lingers
To soon complete THE SEAWITCH
There's so very little hope
And given his liver
With what else can he cope?
Oh, and thank you for the check
Which Alistair will cash tomorrow
But if he delivers no story
Your boss shall have sorrows"

I did feel so helpless
From the very start, mission failed
Then I caught sight of the Scotsman
From the bedroom he hailed

With a cane and a limp
A sudden entrance he made
He looked me up and down
My presence he weighed

"Hello, Mr. Davids
I've been expecting you so
Paul Kohner just called
He keeps close watch, you know
He said you have a review
Of my very first book
If you don't mind, young man
I'd like to have a look"

As I sat by in silence
Watching all the while
Impressed Alistair was
He nodded with a slight smile

"Well done, my young friend"
Said he when he'd read
And digested and swallowed
Every word the review said

"You may call me Alistair
Forego calling me Mister MacLean
Of all male writers in this world
I have the maximum fame
More books have I sold
Than any other who breathes
Except Agatha Christie
And me that woman does peeve
So why in all the world over
Be there no male writer like me?
Because when I was a lad
I went straight off to sea
In the British Navy I fought
From me much could you learn
I caused the Nazis grave horrors
Their ships I did burn
THE SEAWITCH I'll finish
In one week or two
But in the meantime
What are we four lads to do?
My nurse she thinks falsely
She's hidden every bottle
If she knew of my stash
My hide she would throttle
But Willem and Zeljko
Care for me quite a bit
So let's all have a wee one
Why not just one tiny sip?"

A WEE ONE WITH ALISTAIR MACLEAN

I gasped with great terror
I knew what he meant
When the rum started flowing
My reputation would be spent

"The work can wait, lad
I'll start typing tomorrow
But if I don't have a wee one
I'll know such a great sorrow"

So a wee one he would have
And his choice was gin
In the closet nearby
A quick glance I did win

Bottles aplenty
On many a shelf
I was beginning to sense
I'd made a fool of myself

But apart from my being a fool
There was grave danger to his liver
His doctors insisted no drinking
The consequences made me shiver

Said Alistair: "What is the matter, young man?
Won't you have some more?
You've just had one wee one
And you look like you're at death's door"

"Oh, thank you, Alistair," said I
"But one wee one's enough
I've known for some years now
That I can't hold my stuff"

"Well, as for me, another wee one"
Said Alistair, quite intent
"And I'll imagine those days here
When Marilyn Monroe paid the rent"

Paul Jeffrey Davids

Zeljko, he had
So little to say
Quiet he was
That was his way

He painted on glass
Delicate and fine
If that glass broke
It would shatter every line

Art is impermanent
That was his rule
To make something to last
Was the art of a fool

Zeljko sipped rather quietly
Willem's gulping was loud
I succumbed to another round
Of me Alistair seemed proud

And so on and on it went
One wee one, then another
And by the very next morning
I was soon to discover
That I'd spent the whole night there
Without calling my wife
She was worried beyond measure
She feared for my life

When Alistair heard me discuss
My bride's enrapturing beauty
He inquired and he pried
To learn much about this cutie

"Ah, son, you have a fine wife
Let's invite her to our party
She must join us tonight
We'll all make a small sortie"

A WEE ONE WITH ALISTAIR MACLEAN

I went to work that day
In fear of what was to come
I had a hangover from gin
And also from rum

Paul Kohner he called me
Into his office quite huge
I was rumpled and confused
I felt like a stooge

"Give me your report," said he
"Let me hear your rendition
Of all the details
Of my client's condition"

I said: "Alistair he is typing"
But I hemmed and I hawed
One thing's for sure
My report was quite flawed

My boss asked: "How many pages
Did he write yesterday?
Is he staying quite sober
And avoiding all play?"

I said: "The SEAWITCH will be brilliant
A story clever and new
Let's trust the great Alistair
He knows what to do
He's inspired by Marilyn
Her memories are very near
Since she died in that house
To Alistair she's quite dear"

Paul Kohner's deep laugh
Shook the whole room
"Is that what he told you?
He must think you're a buffoon!"

"Marilyn Monroe did not die there"
Paul Kohner said
"It was all the way across town
Where she was found dead"

As I knocked on Alistair's door again
How I felt like a fool
Was I so gullible
And being used like a tool?

They invited me in
And soon showed me the stash
Willem now had a briefcase
Stuffed with cash

Ten thousand dollars
Every dollar was there
Alistair planned some fun
He'd take us somewhere

He called this mad money
Just a keen little spark
He was worth so many millions
He'd spend this on a lark

Before my wife arrived
We drank wine somewhat stale
And I challenged his story
I challenged the tale

He said: "Of course Marilyn died here!"
Alistair was quite stern
"Paul Kohner knows nothing about it
And that I confirm
Her death here was hushed up
By false media hype
There was a big cover-up
The lies were so ripe"

A WEE ONE WITH ALISTAIR MACLEAN

Then it was time for a wee one
And another just for fun
But when Hollace arrived
She wanted dinner not rum

Alistair was quite taken
With my wife's manner quixotic
As he beheld Hollace
He found her exotic

Hollace's hunger
Took center stage
Choosing the right restaurant
Became quite the rage
Willem tried first
Naming this one and that
"The Cock and Bull or Brown Derby
Or Musso and Frank's, how's that?"

"Top of the Mark" said Alistair
"That's where we must go
San Francisco at night
Will be all aglow
It's only four hundred miles
So for a limo you'll now call
We'll fly at once by first class
We'll all have a ball"

We reached San Francisco
In less than two hours
To go straight to the Mark Hopkins
And perhaps take quick showers

Tony was our limo driver
In San Francisco
Willem carried the briefcase
With all of that dough

Tony was an Italian
With splendid good looks
But the reason Alistair liked him?
Tony had read all of his books

Alistair asked: "Which one takes the prize?
 THE GUNS OF NAVARONE, was that my best?
Or FEAR IS THE KEY?
Or THE WAY TO DUSTY DEATH?"

Tony said: "My favorite of all
Was the one you wrote late
Your most recent is your best one
I mean THE GOLDEN GATE"

Said Alistair: "Of all of the landmarks
In this brave land
The Golden Gate Bridge
Is where I'll make my last stand
From that bridge majestic
Overlooking the sea
A man suddenly becomes
All he's meant to be"

At long last to the Top of the Mark
We had all come
But Alistair stopped off in his room
For a tiny wee one

As for the last few steps
To the Top of the Mark
Alistair lost his footing
It was rather dark

He took a small spill
Spraining his ankle
Getting back to his feet
Was all he could handle

A WEE ONE WITH ALISTAIR MACLEAN

To the Maitre d'
He turned with a wave
And in one quick gesture
Thousands of dollars he gave

Said he: "For everyone here
This meal is my treat
I am Alistair MacLean
And I can't be beat!"

By "everyone" he meant
Not just those at the bar
His wave swept the whole restaurant
Those both near and far

The meal was sumptuous
The wine was the best
But for Alistair's liver
That evening was a test

He looked a bit yellow
And purple and green
Seasick and confused
He made quite a scene

The next morning we were awakened
By a telephone call
It was Paul Kohner from Los Angeles
And I couldn't stall

He asked: "What happened last night?
And how is it conceivable?
That you are at the Mark Hopkins Hotel
And therefore not retrievable?
There is much work here
For you to accomplish
And by the way
What about THE SEAWITCH?"

My neck grew sweaty
My face was bright red
At that embarrassing instant
I felt rather dead

"Forgive me Mister Kohner
But what could I do?
Your client kidnapped me
And my wife too
Under protest we flew
To San Francisco
On the next plane we'll return
We want you to know"

Notwithstanding my promise
The next plane we could not take
It was out of the question
Because Tony was late
And Alistair insisted
That without further delay
We zoom off to the Golden Gate
While the day was underway

Across the glorious bridge
We drove once and drove twice
Then five times and six times
It was all rather nice

Ten times we traversed
That bridge of majesty
But I feared my employment
Might become a tragedy

As the sun sank in the west
We departed the bridge at last
And set forth for Sausalito
Where Alistair spent sums vast

A WEE ONE WITH ALISTAIR MACLEAN

Into art galleries extraordinary
Of every conceivable type
Thousands of dollars did he spend
But the evening was ripe

Dinner by the wharf
Looking out at the sea
That's when Alistair MacLean
Had very serious words with me

"Son, if it's a writer
You wish to become
Then listen to me carefully
And I'll tell you how it's done
I cannot type at sixty
Or even forty words a minute
But as for each of my stories
I hurl myself into it
I type with two fingers
I never learned the rules
But what I say far surpasses
Those superficial tools
The typewriter is just an extension
Of my very precise mind
I live for suspense and conflict
And adventures locked in time
My books sell millions the world over
More than I can ever know
Royalties flow into bank accounts
In countries high and low
But a bad word never should you write
Keep your writing clean
My grandmother never would blush
At what I write and mean"

I saw Alistair a few times again
He departed "Marilyn Monroe's" home
And moved to where Boris Karloff once lived
To finish writing his tome

Paul Jeffrey Davids

Boris Karloff of FRANKENSTEIN
Who played dozens of creatures
His old house was a bit frightening
Like all of his movie features

The Karloff house I feared might end
Alistair's life and thus the tale
For the stairway was equipped
With neither handhold nor a rail

I thought a wee one or maybe two
In the middle of the night
Would cause a fall from those stone steps
Toppling Alistair one whole flight

But I was wrong, he lived to finish
THE SEAWITCH and eight books more
He was a master to the end
Creating exciting lore

THE SEAWITCH they declined to film
At Columbia Studio
The young executives thought it was
Altogether too macho

They wanted a female hero
And changes from beginning to end
More action and character
The whole thing they did upend

Alistair brushed them off
He knew he was the best
And of some of the young executives
He said: "I'm tempted to call them pests"

"Let them sell a hundred million books
And then tell me how to write
At least they paid me very well
Though they've buried it out of sight"

A WEE ONE WITH ALISTAIR MACLEAN

Once he told us in a voice quite sober
"Surely you'll have a baby before I've died
Remember me when that day comes
A godfather I'll be with pride"

When that day came he could not be found
Switzerland had become his land
He was quite incommunicado
No longer a guiding hand

Alistair kept drinking wee ones
Soon his liver could no longer last
He died quite young in the scheme of things
At sixty-four he suddenly he passed

It was nineteen eighty-seven
February 2nd, I do confess
Two days before my birthday
He went the way to dusty death

Paul Kohner, the Magician of Sunset Boulevard, who opened the door for me to work in Hollywood and who later enabled me to join the Writers Guild of America by acting as my agent for assignments with Cornel Wilde and Carlo Ponti.

Young Paul Kohner (left) introduces Albert Einstein to Carl Laemmle (founder of Universal Pictures).

Ernest Hemingway (left) with film agent/producer Paul Kohner (right).

Zeljko Primerl (left), Willem (center) and I'm at the right. We're in front of the car that drove us around San Francisco with Alistair MacLean (1976).

I'm with (and behind) Alistair MacLean in San Francisco (1976).

My wife, Hollace Davids, with Alistair MacLean (1976).

Paul Kohner in front of the Paul Kohner Agency on Sunset Boulevard, where I worked from 1976 to 1981.

Hollace and I are with Alistair MacLean (right) 1976.

133

31. DON'T ASK A POET

If facts you crave
On topics obscure
That few men appreciate
Or can endure

If scientific clarity
Is your only care
With precision quite perfect
Mathematics takes you there

And if knowledge arcane
From dusty centuries gone by
Calls out to you
Without making you sigh

And answers you need
That will never waver
Then listen well, my friend
I'll do you a favor

Don't ask a poet
Because a poet won't know it
No, don't ask a poet
Because a poet can't show it

And if you would build
An edifice tall
With elevators fast
And offices big and small

Or if you would design
A rocket for space
Don't ask a poet
A poet has no place

DON'T ASK A POET

Nor should you consult a poet
If you will make a great ship
Or a train or a car
That needs no gas for a trip

Or if you want a faster computer
With a million gigabytes
Or a new modern city
With ten billion lights

Don't ask a poet
Because a poet can't hoe it
No, don't ask a poet
A poet would blow it

But if what you seek
Is ethereal, unseen
By all of the people
Who forgot how to dream

If you need inspiration
That comes from above
If you crave a new vision
That is filled with love

If artistic persuasion
Calls out to your heart
Then listen well, my friend
If you want to be smart

Go ask a poet
A poet will show it
Find yourself the best poet
A poet will know it

About the Author

Growing up in Kensington and Bethesda, Maryland, I set my sights on working in film and television by age ten when I was an amateur filmmaker (of fantasy films with dinosaurs, dragons, sea serpents and other creatures) and an avid reader of Famous Monsters of Filmland magazine. I was a young teenage winner in the magazine's amateur filmmaking contest, sponsored by editor Forry Ackerman, who encouraged my ambition for a career in entertainment. After graduating from Princeton University with a major in psychology, I was one of fifteen students accepted to study on a graduate fellowship at the American Film Institute Center for Advanced Film Studies in its opening year at Greystone in Beverly Hills. Some of my fellow students were David Lynch, Terrence Malick, Caleb Deschanel, Jeremy Kagan, Matthew Robbins and Tom Rickman. While at AFI, I made a short film entitled EXAMINATION, based on a story I wrote at Princeton that won the university's Tiger Magazine Humorous Writing Award.

While on an AFI internship on a Warner Brothers film called DEALING, I met Hollace Goodman. We were strangers passing on a street in Cambridge, Massachusetts. The fact that we stopped for a moment to talk changed the course of our lives. We discovered we had gone to rival high schools and shared interests. About a year later, we were married and lived in an apartment on the beach in Marina del Rey, California.

I got my first break in film working for renowned agent Paul Kohner as his script reader. To help cover my salary, he arranged for me to work part time for director William Wyler, who needed help preparing to receive the AFI Life Achievement Award. Paul Kohner also got me into the WGA, writing for actor/director Cornel Wilde, and Carlo Ponti and Terrence Young. I also worked for my idol, producer/director George Pal.

I helped produce the original TRANSFORMERS animated television series. My credit as production coordinator for Marvel Productions appears on 79 episodes of TRANSFORMERS, and I wrote some of them, too, including TF classics such as COSMIC RUST, THIEF IN THE NIGHT, CHAOS and GRIMLOCK'S NEW BRAIN.

My film credits as writer, producer and/or director include:
SHE DANCES ALONE with Bud Cort and Max von Sydow
Showtime's ROSWELL: THE UFO COVERUP
TIMOTHY LEARY'S DEAD, a biography of LSD guru Leary

STARRY NIGHT, a fantasy about Vincent van Gogh
THE ARTIST & THE SHAMAN, my personal journey as an artist
THE SCI-FI BOYS – Peter Jackson surveys film effects history
JESUS IN INDIA, exploring the eighteen "missing years" of Jesus
BEFORE WE SAY GOODBYE, a Hispanic-American story
…and my latest: THE LIFE AFTER DEATH PROJECT, a feature documentary study of the evidence for life after death.

A few years after we were married, Hollace left her career in psychology and teaching children with learning disabilities, and she too entered the entertainment field. Over the years, she became one of Hollywood's most noted special event experts and has served as Vice-President of Columbia Pictures, Sony Pictures and TriStar Pictures, and for over fifteen years she has been Senior Vice-President of Special Projects for Universal Pictures. She handles all the premieres of Universal's major features.

THE FIRES OF PELE: MARK TWAIN'S LEGENDARY LOST JOURNAL was my first book, co-written with Hollace, with a Foreword by Stan Lee, an introduction by Forrest J Ackerman and artistic contributions from Sergio Aragones.

In the 1990's, Hollace and I co-wrote a series of STAR WARS books for Lucasfilm and Bantam/Random House, including THE GLOVE OF DARTH VADER, THE LOST CITY OF THE JEDI, ZORBA THE HUTT'S REVENGE, MISSION FROM MOUNT YODA, QUEEN OF THE EMPIRE and PROPHETS OF THE DARK SIDE. The books sold millions of copies worldwide in many languages.

In addition to writing novels and poetry and creating films, I am an artist. I create oil paintings, pen and ink drawings, and pastels. My art has been showcased in major galleries, and you can visit my online art gallery at www.pauldavids.com

From PROFESSOR HACK HARDDRIVE'S™ POEMS, I created humorous songs, which are available on the Internet. Other of my comedy songs include YOU'RE THINNER, YOU'RE FATTER and WE LOVE YOU, WE HATE YOU, which are also included as poems in this book.

My more serious poems appear in RIGHT-BRAINED POEMS FOR LEFT-BRAINED PEOPLE. Another of my books of humorous poetry is: POEMS TO READ WHEN YOU RUN OUT OF WEED.

Hollace Davids and I are residents of Los Angeles and Big Bear Lake, California, and we also spend much time in Santa Fe, New Mexico and Sedona, Arizona, where I love to paint the Southwest.

HIGHLIGHTS OF THE JOURNEY

In 2007, Hollace Davids and I received the Saturn Award for Best DVD of 2006 for the feature documentary THE SCI-FI BOYS, distributed by Universal Pictures Home Entertainment and NBC Universal Television. The Saturn Award is presented by the Academy of Science-Fiction, Fantasy and Horror in Hollywood.

My daughter, Jordan Duvall (left), and I are dressed to depart for the Academy Awards.

I'm with my son, Scott M. Davids, a Hollywood feature film editor and President of a digital effects company he founded, Level 256, Inc.

I won Princeton University's three top writing awards in one year while in my junior year, including the Morris Croll Poetry Prize (shared), the F. Scott Fitzgerald Prize for Creative Writing (donated by Charles Scribners' Sons Publishers) and the Tiger Magazine Award for Humorous Writing. Medical school plans were abandoned to pursue cinema at the American Film Institute Center for Advanced Film Studies in its opening year.

I'm directing my American Film Institute half-hour student film, EXAMINATION, and I'm with actor Paul Picerni (famous for the TV series THE UNTOUCHABLES) who starred in it.

My portrait of 1960's psychedelic pioneer Timothy Leary toward the end of his life, painted after I produced and directed the film TIMOTHY LEARY'S DEAD.

Part of my TIMES SQUARE tryptych that was on display outdoors for three years at the entrance to Cafe Tu Tu Tango at Universal City Walk in Los Angeles.

Another of my more whimsical paintings, this one called HOLLYWOOD PRODUCERS ON SKIS.

One of my larger paintings with a science-fiction flair, called
NEW YORK WOMEN IN SPACE (2001).

Hollywood Foreign Press Association

Certificate of Nomination for Award

Be it known that

Roswell

was nominated for a Golden Globe Award of Merit
for Outstanding Achievement for

Best Mini-Series or Motion Picture Made for Television

This judgment being rendered with reference to Television
which have qualified for consideration by the
Hollywood Foreign Press Association during the year ending 1994

PRESIDENT

EXECUTIVE SECRETARY

I'm on the set of the 1994 Showtime Film ROSWELL, starring Kyle MacLachlan, Martin Sheen and Dwight Yoakam. I was executive producer and co-writer of the story.

Paul Jeffrey Davids on Davids Lane in the Hamptons, New York (2008).

One of my favorites of my pen and ink drawings:
"Ducks in Central Park" from 1999.

As I look today, in my chaotic office where I am busy editing my video performances of these and other humorous poems, to be released on DVD and also as an audiobook.

I'm at the right, in makeup and costume as Professor Hack HardDrive, alongside Ron James (left) who provided the green-screen studio for videotaping my poetic performances. Ron James is in macabre makeup to play my tattoo artist in the video. I have a "Loraine" tattoo on my forehead for the poem MY TATTOOS, which appears in POEMS TO READ WHEN YOU RUN OUT OF WEED.

This is another of my poses in make-up and costume as Professor Hack HardDrive.

I'm with the alien prop from my Showtime film ROSWELL. The alien remains beside my desk in my home office.

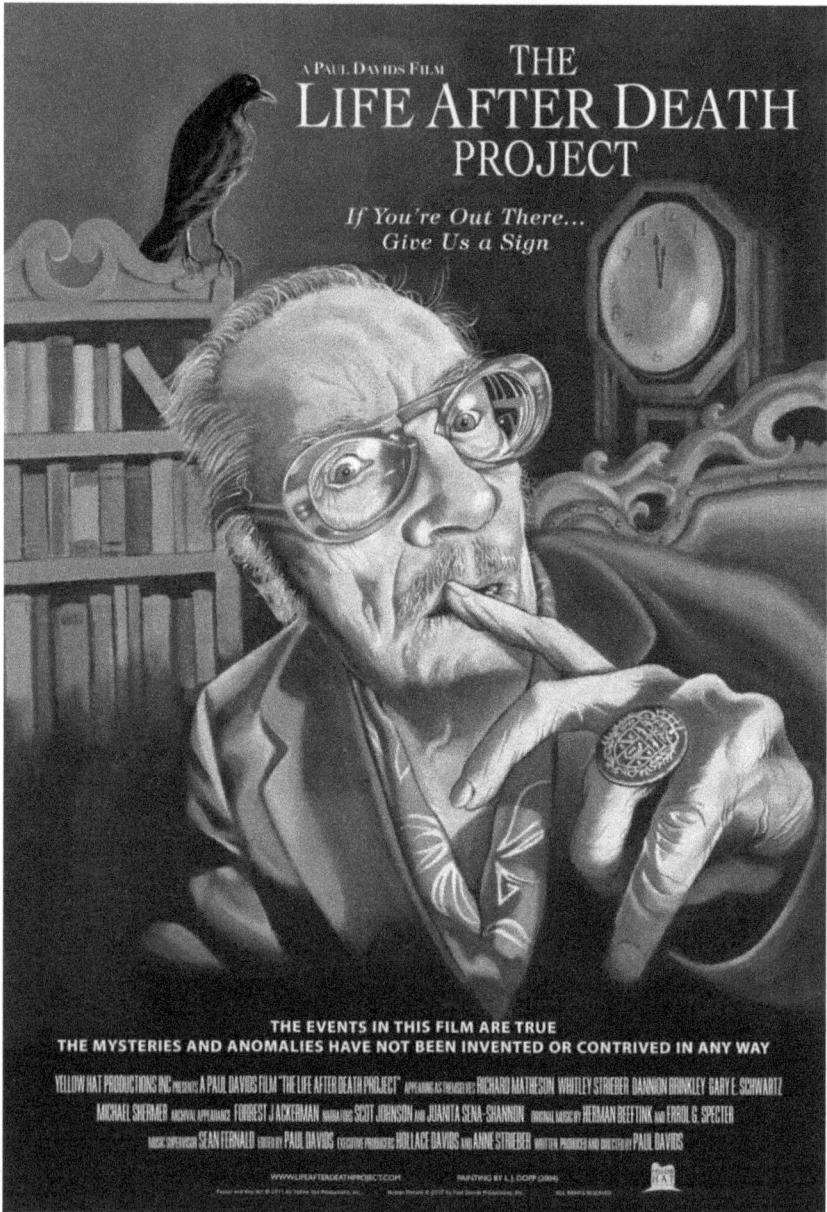

The poster for my new feature documentary which examines evidence for life after
death: *THE LIFE AFTER DEATH PROJECT*

RIGHT-BRAINED POEMS
FOR LEFT-BRAINED PEOPLE

Paul Jeffrey Davids

*A book of my serious poetry. The cover is my self-portrait in Paris,
an oil painting from 2011.*

POEMS TO READ
WHEN YOU RUN OUT OF WEED

Paul Jeffrey Davids

Another of my books of humorous poems. The painting is one of my oil paintings from 2005 entitled "The Sundance Kids."

Printed in the United States of America

www.ingramcontent.com/pod-product-compliance
Lightning Source LLC
Chambersburg PA
CBHW021333090426
42742CB00008B/587